Palgrave Studies in Economic History

Series Editor
Kent Deng, London School of Economics, London, UK

Palgrave Studies in Economic History is designed to illuminate and enrich our understanding of economies and economic phenomena of the past. The series covers a vast range of topics including financial history, labour history, development economics, commercialisation, urbanisation, industrialisation, modernisation, globalisation, and changes in world economic orders.

More information about this series at
http://www.palgrave.com/gp/series/14632

James Greenhalgh

Injurious Vistas: The Control of Outdoor Advertising, Governance and the Shaping of Urban Experience in Britain, 1817–1962

palgrave
macmillan

James Greenhalgh
University of Lincoln
Lincoln, UK

ISSN 2662-6497 ISSN 2662-6500 (electronic)
Palgrave Studies in Economic History
ISBN 978-3-030-79017-2 ISBN 978-3-030-79018-9 (eBook)
https://doi.org/10.1007/978-3-030-79018-9

This Palgrave Macmillan imprint is published by the registered company Springer Nature Switzerland AG
The registered company address is: Gewerbestrasse 11, 6330 Cham, Switzerland

Acknowledgements

There are a lot of people who should be thanked for helping with this book. Barry Doyle, some years ago, suggested that there was more to advertising control than I might have allowed during the last minute of a question session in Telford, and this is where this book began. That conference took place under the auspices of the Urban History Group—whose members and participants have been a source of ideas and support over the years—and thus, the Economic History Society and the research for this book was funded by the EHS Carnevali Grant, for which I am very grateful. I would also like to thank Oliver Hilliam and the CPRE for their permission to use the images they inherited from SCAPA, as well as everyone at the London Met Archives and the History of Advertising Trust who helped me. Michele Vescovi, Ed and Lisa Owens, Maarten Walraven and Sheona Davies helped in the translation of various languages. Jack Head found elusive pieces of legislation and Tracy Davis kindly shared her work on the Zaeo scandal. Otto Saumarez Smith helped with some references and invited me to talk on this subject at SPUD, which has proved a great environment for urban discussions over the years. Alistair Kefford talked to me about private property and land value, and Guy Ortolano shared ideas about social democracy and market liberalism. David Ibitson helped me with some Victorian culture. Simon Gunn, Leif Jerram and Charlotte Wildman read very early versions of this and were encouraging as were the University of Lincoln modern history group who read several sections and chapters. Richard Rodger lent his encyclopaedic knowledge of Scottish urban government via Zoom, which allowed me to explore the importance of understanding this story from a British rather than merely an English perspective. Katrina Navickas shared research and, just as importantly, disagreed with me about liberal governmentality, whilst Tom Hulme and John Davis both helped me with sources on local government. Kim Byeongkwan offered wisdom on what seemed like a daily basis. Katherine Fennelly provided crucial insight into heritage legislation and the history of improvement, and was constantly supportive and interested, as she always is, and this book is for her.

Contents

Abbreviations

AMC	Association of Municipal Councils
ARA	Advertisements Regulation Act
ASRA	Advertising Stations (Rating) Act
BPAA	British Poster Advertising Association
CPRE	Council for the Preservation of Rural England
CPS	Commons Protection Society
HTPA	Housing, Town Planning Act
MT&CP	Ministry of Town and Country Planning
SCAPA	Society for Checking the Abuses of Public Advertising
T&CPA	Town and Country Planning Act
UBA	United Billposters Association
UKBPA	United Kingdom Billposters' Association

List of Figures

CHAPTER 1

Introduction

Abstract This chapter introduces the book as a history of how outdoor advertising was positioned, challenged and regulated principally as a physical and experiential phenomenon. It argues that the few histories of advertising in existence have failed to examine the causes and meanings of the disagreements over the place of outdoor advertising in modern Britain. It is concerned with the development and application of primarily legislative and governmental approaches to controlling commercial signage, billboards, posters and hoardings of various types in both the countryside and urban areas and their development between the early-nineteenth century and the beginning of the 1960s. As such, what follows can be read in basic form as a narrative of the campaigns, bills and byelaws that radically curtailed the proliferation of outdoor advertising over a century and a half, but is also a means to examine the character of governmental approaches to the regulation of urban and rural spaces and the meanings attached to them.

Keywords Posters · Billboards · Capitalism · Space · Governance

J. Greenhalgh, *Injurious Vistas: The Control of Outdoor Advertising, Governance and the Shaping of Urban Experience in Britain, 1817–1962*, Palgrave Studies in Economic History,
https://doi.org/10.1007/978-3-030-79018-9_1

It has been common for histories of advertising to begin with the assertion that posters and signage extoling the virtues of certain goods and services are perhaps as old as commerce itself.[1] As advertising executive and writer David Bernstein asserted in 1997, 'advertising began outdoors' and might plot its linage from 'inscriptions on Egyptian monuments' to the first flowering of modern advertising as genuine 'art' in the evocative posterage of fin-de-siècle Paris.[2] In drawing these somewhat tenuous links between the ancient past and contemporary modes of advertising, Bernstein echoed a longer tradition of historicising outdoor advertising that itself stretched back a century and a half. In 1866, Larwood and Hotten's *History of Signboards* pointed to evidence from ancient Egypt, Greece and Rome to suggest that placards advertising everything from wine to gladiatorial contests were as ubiquitous in classical civilisation as they had become by the middle of the nineteenth century.[3] In 1905, Clarence Moran's *The Business of Advertising* claimed that 'at every stage of the world's history advertisement has been the inseparable handmaid of commerce', whilst by 1937, former British Poster Advertising Association (BPAA) president, Cyril Sheldon claimed that 'the poster, in some form or other, is almost as old as civilisation'.[4]

The implication is that outdoor advertising had been a vital, indeed inseparable part of economic function since time immemorial was one of the most common bastions upon which advertisers and billposting companies founded their defence of the profession. However, despite continuing efforts to locate the progenitor of the billboard in the markets and bazaars of the distant past, in the visual language of modern culture outdoor advertising represents a brand of modernity rooted in the most spectacular forms of nineteenth- and twentieth-century capitalism. Times Square, Shibuya Crossing and Piccadilly Circus, with their towering,

[1] This is common to many histories of advertising, for example, see: Clarence Moran, *The Business of Advertising* (Abingdon, 1905), pp. 20–24; Cyril Sheldon, *A History of Poster Advertising* (London, 1937), p. 1. In the rather more neutral Blanche B. Elliott, *The History of English Advertising* (London, 1962), she suggests that whilst playbills might reasonably date to the thirteenth century the poster craze was a phenomenon of the early nineteenth century.

[2] David Bernstein, *Advertising Outdoors: Watch This Space!* (London, 1997), pp. 14–25.

[3] Jacob Larwood and John Camden Hotten, *The History of Signboards, from the Earliest Times to the Present Day* (London, 1908 [1866]), pp. 1–3.

[4] Moran, *The Business of Advertising*, p. 98; Sheldon, *A History of Poster Advertising*, p. 1.

illuminated billboards are emblematic of the simultaneously thrilling and bewildering urban modernity of New York, Tokyo and London, respectively. Conversely, when film directors sought to realise dystopian, often futuristic cityscapes across the twentieth century— in Fritz Lang's *Metropolis*, John Carpenter's *They Live* or *Blade Runner's* Los Angeles— they did so by depicting the vast scale, intrusiveness and inescapability of advertising in urban environments. If, as Thomas Richards argued, from the mid-nineteenth century, the commodity became the 'focal point of all representation, the dead centre of the modern world', then outdoor advertising was its most potent material manifestation.[5]

The impulse to assert the long continuity of outdoor advertising that is evidenced in a century and a half of histories is, then, more than merely an attempt to lend an air of venerable antiquity to the advertising profession. Instead, what the likes of Sheldon and Moran sought to do was to purposefully confront an opposition that, from its emergence in the late nineteenth century, depicted poster and, later, billboard advertising as a distinctly modern and largely undesirable product of the growing mass market. Proponents of outdoor advertising control placed their objections to posters and signs at a nexus of emerging concerns over the ways that capitalism, expanding commercial cultures and new technologies of display disrupted the experience of the modern world. In Britain, Richardson Evans—who would go on to become the highest-profile advocate of legislative controls on outdoor advertising—encapsulated the concerns over advertising's distinctive relationship to modernity in 1890, observing that the 'march of disfigurement' need not be 'absolutely or universally accepted as the inexorable law of progress'.[6] Indeed, when famed architect Alfred Waterhouse wrote to *The Times* in November 1892, he lamented the 'modern advertising mania…the disease [that] has gone far to destroy the appearance of our towns' adding that even 'the very loveliest spots in our island… are being degraded by this wanton vulgarity'.[7] Opposition to outdoor advertising was, though,

[5] Thomas Richards, *The Commodity Culture of Victorian England: Advertising and Spectacle, 1851–1914* (Stanford, 1990), p. 1.

[6] Richardson Evans, *The Age of Disfigurement* (London, 1893), p. 1. Evans was the driving force behind the Society for Checking the Abuses of Public Advertising (SCAPA), who emerged in the late nineteenth century as the primary opponents of outdoor advertising. Their origins and activities are dealt with in Chapters 3 and 4.

[7] *The Times*, 18 November 1892, p. 10.

never a simple matter of anti-modernity, nor an entirely unified cause with a single origin.[8] It was a slow-burning conflict that changed in character and in characters over the decades, mirroring the complexities of shifting attitudes towards how commercial concerns, governmental authority and citizens' experience of daily life interacted in both urban and rural settings.

This book examines the causes and meanings of the disagreements over the place of outdoor advertising in modern Britain that so occupied the energies and inkwells of activists like Evans and Waterhouse. It is concerned with the development and application of primarily legislative and governmental approaches to controlling commercial signage, billboards, posters and hoardings of various types in both the countryside and urban areas and their development between the early nineteenth century and the beginning of the 1960s. As such, what follows can be read in basic form as a narrative of the campaigns, bills and byelaws that radically curtailed the proliferation of outdoor advertising over a century and a half. However, this book is not a history of the content nor forms of outdoor advertising. There is little discussion of the techniques of billboard advertisers and scant examination of the developing technologies of print or illumination. Nor is there a great deal of attention paid to the regulation of the claims and character of advertisements themselves, excepting where laws that governed content intersected with other aspects of control. What is on the billboard or the poster are concerns for other histories. Instead, the control of outdoor advertising is studied here as a means to examine the changing character of how lived spaces were understood and governed in modern Britain. It begins with the first attempts to curtail the spread of bills and signboards in the early nineteenth century, tracks the way advertising control reflected changing patterns of urban governance and thus concludes in decades following the Second World War with the establishment of a series of laws and regulatory attitudes that radically altered the visual environment of British towns and cities.

This is, then, a history of how outdoor advertising was positioned, challenged and regulated principally as a physical and experiential phenomenon, and what makes this topic such a useful vehicle for a

[8] James Taylor, 'Written in the Skies: Advertising, Technology and Modernity in Britain Since 1885', *Journal of British Studies* 55:4 (2016), pp. 750–780; Paul Readman 'Landscape Preservation, "Advertising Disfigurement", and English National Identity c.1890–1914', *Rural History* 12:1 (2001), pp. 61–83.

more wide-reaching study of space and its governance is a certain duality. Outdoor advertising has consistently been an accepted, even vital part of the economic fabric and functions of a modern society, yet it has often been simultaneously reviled for its distinctly material ability to disrupt the use and even 'value' of rural and urban environments alike. Moreover, the opposition to outdoor advertising was shaped and reframed over time, reflecting the shifting priorities and views of a cast of influential actors and organisations. As we shall see, outdoor advertisements were, amongst other things, a very physical nuisance to those seeking to improve nineteenth-century cities, at the intersection of discourses of public space, public health and liberal governance by the end of the century, a tantalising though slippery source of rateable revenue for local authorities, and represented a challenge to urban planners' ambitions during the post-war period. Yet, only the most vociferous opponents ever doubted that outdoor advertising had a place in the normal commercial functioning of British society. Nor, conversely, did the majority of advertisers and poster companies—at least after the middle of the nineteenth century—believe that there should not be limits on the location or size of outdoor advertisements. Here, the continually contested status of outdoor advertising reveals the timbre of much larger debates about rural and urban space, the commercialisation of everyday life, planning, national identity and social class.

Despite its emphasis on outdoor advertising's potential to illuminate other debates, at its heart this book also evidences a radical change in the character of both rural and urban environments that has been largely forgotten in twenty-first-century Britain. It tracks a story of how opposition to poster advertising gathered momentum as the practice itself increased in profusion from the early part of the nineteenth century. Beginning with the emergence of the advertising station in the mid-nineteenth century, new printing technology and the growth of the mass market drove the proliferation of larger hoardings and billboards that superseded billposting as the dominant form of outdoor advertising by the start of the interwar period.[9] Images from before the Second World War evidence the volume and size of advertisements on streets, rural roads and railway sidings, shop fronts and gable ends (see Figs. 1.1, 1.2

[9] Bernstein, *Advertising Outdoors*, p. 12; W. Hamish Fraser, *The Coming of the Mass Market, 1850–1914* (London, 1981); Ernest Turner, *The Shocking History of Advertising* (London, 1965), p. 242.

Fig. 1.1 Advertising on the front of a house, Wandsworth, 1930s (*Source* Author's original)

Fig. 1.2 Row of Shops, Balls Pond Rd, Hackney, 1930s (*Source* Author's original)

Fig. 1.3 Hoardings outside GWR Station, Liverpool, c.1910 (*Source* Author's original)

and 1.3). The book deals with the reaction to this commercialisation of everyday spaces. It is a story of how activism, public opinion and legislation began, through long efforts, to curtail and eliminate much of the outdoor advertising in Britain. Indeed, it is perhaps testament to how successful the opposition to outdoor advertising was that the 'ghost sign' (see Fig. 1.4) is now consumed by heritage tours and urban explorers as a nostalgic curio of an unfamiliar past and that the importance of such a significant development in the visual environment has been largely forgotten by historians of modern Britain.[10]

The practice and content of advertising has, of course, been of considerable interest to historians, who have shown how its development raised questions over everything from the cost to consumers to the intrusion of the nakedly commercial into the everyday lives and homes of readers, listeners and viewers as technologies developed.[11] Indeed, Sean Nixon's

[10] Stefan Schutt, Sam Roberts and Leanne White (eds), *Advertising and Public Memory: Social, Cultural and Historical Perspectives and Ghost Signs* (Abingdon, 2017).

[11] Stuart Ewen, *Captains of Consciousness: Advertising and the Social Roots of Consumer Culture* (New York, 1976); Matthew Hilton, *Consumerism in Twentieth-Century Britain*

Fig. 1.4 A 'Ghost Sign', Central London, 2019 (*Source* Author's original)

examination of the reservations over television advertising and 'commercial persuasion' in the home parallels similar questions raised about the

(Cambridge, 2003), chapter 7; Sean Nixon, *Hard Sell: Advertising, Affluence and Transatlantic Relations, c.1951–69* (Manchester, 2013); Clemens Wischermann and Elliott Shore (eds), *Advertising and the European City: Historical Perspectives* (Aldershot, 2000).

presence of billboards on residential streets in Chapter 5 of this book.[12] Debates in this body of scholarship nevertheless tend to revolve around the methods and strategies of advertising—focusing on, for example, the Americanisation of advertising techniques, the application of ever-more-sophisticated theories of consumer manipulation and the potential of advertising content to reveal certain constructions of gender and family—whilst questions about its control are largely fixed on the regulation of manufacturers' claims about their products.[13] Thomas Richards' study of the relationship between advertising and spectacular capitalism is important here not because of its disputed conclusions about the creation of a middle-class commodity culture—marketing of commodities in various forms had existed since at least the middle of the eighteenth century[14]—but because Richards recognises the shock caused by the sheer volume and material intrusiveness of outdoor advertising as it emerged in the early nineteenth-century city.[15]

Opposition to outdoor advertising was only ever partially framed by reference to its content and techniques. As Aron Segal has demonstrated in nineteenth-century Paris, there was considerable concern about the disruptive qualities of outdoor advertisements as a spatial component of the urban landscape, especially from early preservationists, which sat alongside concerns over the effects of the messages posters contained.[16] In twentieth-century America, both Kurt Iveson and Laura Baker have observed that objections to outdoor advertisements from planners were

[12] Nixon, *Hard Sell*, p. 182.

[13] Fraser, *The Coming of the Mass Market*, pp. 134–146; Frank Mort, 'The Commercial Domain: Advertising and the Cultural Management of Demand', in Becky Conekin, Frank Mort and Chris Waters (eds), *Moments of Modernity: Reconstructing Britain, 1945–1964* (London, 1999), pp. 55–75.

[14] For example: Neil McKendrick, John Brewer and J.H. Plumb, *The Birth of the Consumer Society: The Commercialization of Eighteenth-Century England* (Bloomington, 1982), p. 141.

[15] Richards, *The Commodity Culture of Victorian England*, introduction. For critics see: Christopher A. Kent's review in *Victorian Periodicals Review* 25:3 (1992), pp. 145–147 and John K. Walton, 'Towns and Consumerism', in Martin Daunton (ed), *The Cambridge Urban History of Britain, Vol. 3 1840–1950* (Cambridge, 2000), pp. 715–744 (pp. 723 and 735).

[16] Aaron J. Segal, 'Commercial Immanence: The Poster and Urban Territory in Nineteenth-Century France', in Wischermann and Shore (eds), *Advertising and the European City*, pp. 113–138 (pp. 129–132).

rooted in the ability of billboards and signs to disrupt the visual uniformity, and thus civic benefits, that they ascribed to their schemes for the built environment.[17] Yet, historians of advertising in Britain, excepting examinations of window displays, have rarely touched upon outdoor advertising from a spatial perspective.[18] Indeed, on the rare occasions where control of outdoor advertising is tackled at all, the tendency has been to position the interventions in the control of outdoor advertising as the product of preservationist campaigns and amenity societies that emerged from the late nineteenth century.[19] However, approaches to the control of outdoor advertising had a much longer and more diverse trajectory. As this book shows, controlling outdoor advertising was bound up with the impulse towards improvement, the emergence of patterns of local government regulation and by the middle of the twentieth century was equally relevant to planners as it was to those who sought to preserve architectural and rural beauty.

Studies of Europe and the USA point to the broader possibilities of the examination of outdoor advertising to illuminate debates about the way modern patterns of governance understood both rural and urban space. This direction is taken up by James Taylor in his study of sky signs and aerial advertisements in nineteenth- and early twentieth-century Britain.[20] Taylor's depiction of attempts to control the advance of advertising techniques into the realm of the sky—by means of building-top steel frames,

[17] Laura Baker, 'Public Sites Versus Public Sights: The Progressive Response to Outdoor Advertising and the Commercialization of Public Space', *American Quarterly* 59:4 (2007), pp. 1187–1213; Kurt Iveson, 'Branded Cities: Outdoor Advertising, Urban Governance, and the Outdoor Media Landscape', *Antipode* 44:1 (2012), pp. 151–174. Also: John W. Houck (ed), *Outdoor Advertising: History and Regulation* (London, 1969); Charles R. Taylor and Weih Chang, 'The History of Outdoor Advertising Regulation in the United States', *Journal of Macromarketing* 15:1 (1995), pp. 47–59.

[18] For example: Charlotte Wildman, *Urban Redevelopment and Modernity in Liverpool and Manchester, 1918–39* (London, 2016), pp. 92–98.

[19] Anne M. Cronin, *Advertising Myths: The Strange Half-Lives and Images of Commodities* (London, 2004), pp. 34–35; Turner, *The Shocking History of Advertising*. The exceptions to the prevailing narrative are two books by former advertising industry professionals Terry Nevett, *Advertising in Britain: A History* (London, 1982)—a book produced on behalf of the advertising industry's own History of Advertising Trust—and Cyril Sheldon, *A History of Poster Advertising* (London, 1937) who both lean quite heavily on the—in reality sometimes rather reluctant—adoption of self-policing by the advertising contractors as the main driver of change.

[20] Taylor, 'Written in the Skies'.

projected light displays and sky writing—shows opponents as far more than anti-modern technophobes, or mere aesthetic snobs, a conclusion echoed by Paul Readman in his examination of SCAPA.[21] Instead, Taylor demonstrates that urbanisation and emerging patterns of commercialism meant that the sky took on a new importance as an aspect of urban space and visual experience, a realm that contemporary opinion cast as too valuable a connection to nature to be imperilled by the technological intrusion of advertising. Taylor's work is important here, not merely for its coverage of a significant episode in the history of outdoor advertising—which I return to in Chapter 3—but because it shows the ways that approaches to the government of lived space were being expressed through opposition to outdoor advertising over half a century. In the following chapters, it is the potential of opposition to outdoor advertising to reveal the ways those who governed or claimed an interest in urban and rural spaces imagined the purposes and function of these environments that makes outdoor advertising control so profitable a case study.

Structure and Approach

The examination of the history of controls on outdoor advertising is thus a means by which we can interrogate the patterns and character of urban governance and the meanings and importance ascribed to different aspects of lived spaces. If there is a central argument, here it is that over the course of the period studied the approaches to controlling outdoor advertising show that an ever-more sophisticated and detailed concept of how space, especially urban space functioned and was experienced, was encoded within the mundane habits of governance. This was a diffuse process, enacted by many unrelated actors over the best part of two centuries and I am wary of trying to impose any overarching argument that wanders too close to teleology. When nineteenth-century ultra-Tories proposed ridding the streets of advertising vans, they were hardly envisaging untrammelled progress towards the imagination of the social-democratic subject I describe in Chapter 5. They were, nevertheless, thinking about how urban space should work and formulating rules to govern it that enshrined a consideration of how lived environments might be made more orderly, healthier and ultimately more pleasant at

[21] Readman 'Landscape Preservation, "Advertising Disfigurement"'.

the heart of techniques of governance. The study of outdoor advertising control is an attempt to shed more light on how mundane processes of regulation worked in between grand schemes for urban redevelopment or vast infrastructural projects and made contact with sweeping reforms to public health or housing provision that have captured so much attention.

This process is tackled in a roughly chronological manner in the following chapters, using time periods that roughly correspond to the development of different views on rural and urban spaces. Chapter 2 opens by detailing the development of outdoor advertising on a significant scale and its opposition during the nineteenth century. The story told here reflects the development of nineteenth-century forms of improvement that sought to create greater order in the streets, particularly focused on London.[22] Governments in the first seventy or so years of the century positioned their objections to advertising as a product of the physical nuisance of unfettered billposting and advertising paraphernalia, and their attempts at control reflected practical concerns about the obstruction of rights of way, alongside the general detritus and degradation caused by the continued accumulation of paper and paste on city walls. As the century wore on, outdoor advertising was challenged by the tendency to try and civilise commercial space, particularly after the 1850s.[23] The creation of the various billposters' associations and trade directories shows the opportunistic pragmatism with which private enterprise adapted to the governmental tendencies of the age to begin the standardisation and consolidation of the outdoor advertising industry.

Chapter 3 shows the development of fledgling local government attempts to regulate advertising, central government beginning to consider what regulation might be appropriate and the development of discourses of opposition that questioned the negative effect of advertising on both the population and forms of architectural display. This period saw outdoor advertising questioned in relation to both developing regimes of local government regulation and framed within bigger questions of civic display, morality and public health at the end of the nineteenth

[22] Paul Slack, *The Invention of Improvement: Information and Material Progress in Seventeenth-Century England* (Oxford, 2015), p. 1; Asa Briggs, *The Age of Improvement, 1783–1867* (London, 2014).

[23] Lynda Nead, *Victorian Babylon* (London, 2000).

century.[24] What emerges is a coherent notion of opposition to advertising that moves it beyond the realms of obstruction and nuisance and begins to consider how it might disrupt, disorder and disfigure urban environments so as to damage the civilising influence of space, encapsulated in notions of governmentality.[25] Chapter 4 examines the outlook of SCAPA from the 1890s to look at how the idea of advertisements as a disfiguring presence was framed within the notion of amenity, both in public discourse and in legal terms. A relatively clear, if unsatisfactory to opponents, interpretation of the place of advertising in towns and cities emerged in the 1907 *Advertisements Regulation Act*, and the language of amenity was enshrined in law as a characteristic to be protected from interference. As a result, the debate over control before 1930 was largely restricted to places which demonstrably possessed amenity. This meant SCAPA and their allies focused their energies on the elimination of advertising in beautiful or historically significant rural and urban space for much of the period, with considerable success. Nevertheless, the chapter demonstrates the weaknesses inherent in the interpretation of the various new laws, which meant that, despite attempts by corporations and councils to push the limits of their powers to control outdoor advertising, advertisers were able to continue with relative freedom in urban spaces.

The final substantive chapter demonstrates the ways that local corporations and councils gained control of the approval of outdoor advertisement through changes in the planning legislation, particularly the 1947 *Town and Country Planning Act (T&CPA)*, but also through a changing set of attitudes to public space in central government. Local corporations expressed their desire to control outdoor advertising within the language of post-war planning, positioning billboards and shop-front advertisements as part of an assortment of visually disruptive and disfiguring commercial clutter to be removed as part of their schemes to make cities more orderly and uniform. In this period, I argue that the state imagined a social-democratic subject who had a right to enjoy everyday environments, particularly residential areas, that were free from commercial intrusion. In doing so, the chapter argues, by the end of the

24 James Chandler, *Explaining Local Government: Local Government in Britain Since 1800* (Manchester, 2007); Barry Doyle, 'The Changing Functions of Urban Government: Councillors, Officials and Pressure Groups', in Martin Daunton (ed), *The Cambridge Urban History of Britain, Vol. 3 1840–1950* (Cambridge, 2000), pp. 287–314.

25 Patrick Joyce, *The Rule of Freedom: Liberalism and the Modern City* (London, 2003).

1950s attitudes to advertising demonstrated the wider acceptance in both national and local government that control of the material and visual environment in a planned, holistic manner was both an important technique of modern governance and a responsibility of the state to its citizens.

The study of outdoor advertising control could, of course, lend itself to long discussions of the technical advancements and advertising techniques. I have, however, devoted very little space to examining the difference between, for example, the advertising station of the 1850s or the hoarding of the 1930s, because, except where indicated, these changes do not seem to have been especially important to those who advocated controlling them. Advertising companies often wrote about the neatness and orderliness of their sites, or the ways that the artistic qualities of good postering could enhance drab areas, but there is very rarely any discussion of these elements of taste in the appeal files of the various Ministries or local governments. As Chapter 5 shows, by the 1950s, central government had grown to abhor advertisers' suggestions that they could improve areas with quality designs. SCAPA and other preservationist and amenity societies' objections were always about the effects of any type of outdoor advertising, although they did reserve a special spot in hell for the sky sign. The quality that opponents consistently cared about was the disruption to the material environment, and only rarely did they mention the size, type or content of outdoor advertisements. The study is British in scope dealing at least in passing with all four nations of the UK-as-is in the twenty-first century, I have omitted evidence from what would become the independent Irish state during the middle years of the study, although I could have selected examples from metropolitan Dublin or rural Carlow that would have shown similar tendencies to those in London or Suffolk. England is not, of course London, but the metropole inevitably led the way with much of the legislation and practices discussed here. There is, nevertheless, still much that shows the importance of provincial and non-urban government in driving change, especially in the later years of the study. Scotland is the subject of much discussion here, especially with regard to the concept of amenity. Indeed, in many ways burghs and cities like Edinburgh, Aberdeen and Elgin were national leaders in protecting their built environment from outdoor signage. The book does not mean to imply that there was not uniqueness in Scottish law or forms of urban and spatial governance, simply that many of the issues common to the rest of the Union were also being experienced by the Scottish, albeit flavoured by the different administrative arrangements in Scotland.

The evidence I have used here comes from a range of different sources and differs by period. The whole piece relies on readings of legislation and comes to conclusions about what these materials might mean. Medievalists are right to caution us that assuming that a law describes how people behave would be like assuming that everyone drives within, or perhaps even precisely at the speed limit.[26] Accordingly, I have tried to pay attention to, for example, the fact that flyposting persisted—and indeed persists—long after the nineteenth-century laws that made it largely illegal were passed, instead using the law and debates over it to analyse the intentions of those enacting it and the ways it was implemented. In Chapters 2 and 3, there is substantial use of newspapers and periodicals, not to access the public mood—a slippery concept at best—but to understand the ways in which debates over outdoor advertising were being framed. In addition, where local and national governmental records are often silent or say little to record the reasons behind decisions made, newspaper coverage of court proceedings, select committees and local authority meetings forms a valuable adjunct to the official sources.

Finally, the voices of the advertising companies and billposters themselves are largely absent here. Cyril Sheldon's work and some extracts from the billposting periodicals give some indication of this side of the story, but they appear here mostly when they contested decisions or appealed to local and central government. This gives them a rather adversarial quality in the material, which I do not think is necessarily reflective of their general conduct. It is certainly true that poster advertising companies and other general commercial interests used their considerable economic power and influence to contest proposed legislative controls. It is also true that there were many poster companies, bill stickers, electric signage companies and others who had little regard for anything but their pockets. By-and-large though, and certainly from the end of the nineteenth century, outdoor advertisers often resisted new legislative controls by encouraging co-operation with local authorities and promoting self-regulation from within the industry itself. Few 'respectable companies' persisted in large-scale advertising in the countryside in the face of the public outcry engendered by preservationist campaigns during

[26] Chris Wickham, *The Inheritance of Rome: A History of Europe from 400 to 1000* (London, 2010), p. 14.

the interwar period, for example, whilst the billposting associations periodically assisted in removing and challenging the more outlandish or offensive forms of advertising when public outcry threatened their reputation. That this is a story of opposition and antagonism simply reflects that it was those moments, not the periods of accord, that generated column inches and correspondence, were debated in parliament and ultimately drove the changes in the law and the regulation of the lived environment that form the basis of the study.

CHAPTER 2

Outdoor Advertising and Improvement in the Nineteenth Century

Abstract This chapter deals with the crystallisation of opposition to outdoor advertising in the first half of the nineteenth century. It argues that the common types of outdoor advertising—largely posters, vans and sandwich boards—caused serious nuisance on urban streets, attracting the ire of local government. Whilst it shows that cultural commentators of the period objected, the chief opposition came from government regimes of improvement that sought to eliminate nuisance and 'civilise' outdoor advertising in a city that was increasingly crowded and disordered. Examples of initial forays into advertising control were thus prosaic, positioning outdoor advertising as a material nuisance in bustling streetscapes, rather than as an aesthetic problem. The chapter also shows the response of the advertising trade, which was to organise and consolidate the industry, promoting the advertising station over less ordered forms of postering to bring them in line with governmental desires to alleviate the chaotic and disruptive nature of outdoor advertising.

Keywords Nuisance · Improvement · Posters · Bill stickers · London

J. Greenhalgh, *Injurious Vistas: The Control of Outdoor Advertising, Governance and the Shaping of Urban Experience in Britain, 1817–1962*, Palgrave Studies in Economic History,
https://doi.org/10.1007/978-3-030-79018-9_2

In the mythology of outdoor advertising, the first years of the 1860s stand as a landmark period for the poster trade in Britain.[1] In these years, according to legend, Leeds advertising man Edward Sheldon helped found the United Kingdom Billposters Association (UKBPA) and pioneered the use of the rented poster site, ushering in a more consolidated, effective and civic-minded era for outdoor advertising. There are reasons to question this account of events: rented 'advertising stations' of various types and ownership were, this chapter shows, relatively common well before the 1860s and seem to have existed since at least the 1840s. Moreover, none of Sheldon's contemporaries seem to have recognised his pivotal role before his grandson Cyril wrote his 1937 history of outdoor advertising.[2] Nevertheless, the foregrounding of Edward Sheldon's putative innovations in advertising histories points to the centrality of these two developments in standardising the practices and organisation of outdoor advertising. Indeed, the transition to stations and hoardings owned or rented by advertising contractors alongside the creation of representative industry bodies was the beginning of a process of homogenisation in commercial postering practices that profoundly altered both the business of and opposition to outdoor advertising over the next hundred years.

Sheldon and his contemporaries, in organising respectable trade bodies—there were several competing organisations with similar aims that came and went over time—and establishing greater control of both where advertisements were displayed and those who posted them, were reacting to broader changes in the way that national and local governments saw and regulated urban space around the middle years of the century. Local government—at first in London, but gradually spreading to the provinces—grew increasingly intolerant of the prevailing modus operandi of the poster industry, the billposter, and sought to curtail their activities. At the same time, advertising vans and sandwich men drew the ire of commentators and law makers alike. Opposition in this period certainly

[1] For example, the History of Advertising Trust cites these as pivotal years in its chronology of advertising history https://www.hatads.org.uk/documents/Chronology.pdf accessed 15 March 2021.

[2] This story seems to have originated in Cyril Sheldon, *A History of Poster Advertising* (London, 1937), pp. 3–4 and been picked up by subsequent historians using Sheldon as a source. Richard Nelson and Anthony Edward Sykes, *Outdoor Advertising: Its Function in Modern Advertising and Marketing* (London, 1953), p. 7 for example.

raised the spectres of the unpleasant moral and psychological impact of advertisements' messages and outlandish claims—a theme reformulated again and again over the years—but outdoor advertisements were objects of scorn because they were a chaotic, unregulated and, most importantly, physical nuisance in the already crowded towns and cities.

From a morass of different objections outdoor advertising was gradually framed by the middle of the century in a general public and governmental discourse around this notion of physical nuisance. In an urban environment where the emphasis was shifting to martialling people and the built environment into smoothly functioning 'civilised' flows of commodity and capital, outdoor advertising was both messy and, in many instances, actively obstructive of foot and road traffic. The chapter thus argues that it was the manner of advertising, its physical presence rather than its content or the practice itself that attracted negative attention and fuelled attempts to regulate it. The second half of the century, in which advertising gradually moved to rented hoardings, advertising stations and specific pieces of street furniture, tells the story of how the advertising industry reacted to the pressures to become a more regulated and 'civilised' aspect of the spatio-economic fabric of cities. Though it might never have been desirable, the middle of the nineteenth century saw outdoor advertising ensconced as an accepted part of the normal economic functions of urban space. During this period, it increased in size, sophistication and artistic endeavour, as well as in profitability for an increasingly consolidated group of contractors. Yet, bringing outdoor advertising into the world of what we might call 'civilised capitalism' meant considering it within new frameworks of municipal legislation. The second half of the story told in this chapter thus concerns the transition from nuisance to a more respectable, but, as the following chapter shows, more precarious position as outdoor advertising attracted the attention of municipal corporations and a growing band of aesthetic opponents.

Public Nuisance: Bill Stickers, Sandwich Men and Advertising Vans

Prior to the first moves towards consolidation of the poster advertising industry in the second half of the century, outdoor advertising was conducted in an almost entirely piecemeal fashion and was rather chaotic.[3] Anyone wishing to advertise an event or product had to issue their posters to printers, which were then circulated to 'external paper hangers', better known as bill stickers, who would paper any convenient wall or flat surface with poster and paste, often over others' recently applied bills.[4] Since bill stickers were independently and circumstantially employed, each competed for the most prominent locations to paste his bills, creating thick layers of overlapping bills as high as their brushes could reach on any vaguely suitable surface. Accordingly, rivalry between these 'knight[s] of the brush' was fierce and their 'disfiguring work was a prominent feature of the metropolis' paying little attention to private property, including people's homes and doors.[5] As the magazine *Punch*—a recurring critic of the spread of outdoor advertising over the next fifty years—punned in 1846, the 'advertising mania' had become so extensive that not content with 'covering all the bridges now with bills and placards. They will be turning the bed of the river next into a series of *"four posters"* [original emphasis]'.[6]

In this early period of outdoor advertising expansion, posters and bills were rarely pictorial and consisted almost exclusively of text. It would not be until the 1871 that Fred Walker produced a poster that contemporary observers considered of 'genuine artistic merit' in Britain—a monochrome woodcut for a production of Willkie Collins' *The Woman in White*—whilst it was not until the 1880s that the pioneering colour lithography of Frenchman Jules Chéret made anything but the most basic images common on British streets.[7] As a result, one strand of contemporary criticism focused upon the messages that advertising contained, what James Dawson Burn called, 'The Language of the Walls'. Though vocal, this variety of denunciation gained little popular traction and principally emanated from a small group of intellectuals who lamented the

[3] Clarence Moran, *The Business of Advertising* (Abingdon, 1905), p. 41.

[4] There are many descriptions of this process Ernest Turner, *The Shocking History of Advertising*, p. 72.

[5] Sheldon, *A History of Poster Advertising*, p. 2.

[6] *Punchor the London Charivari* (hereafter '*Punch*'), 1 August 1846, p. 46.

[7] Turner, *The Shocking History of Advertising*, pp. 98–99.

supposed malign societal influence of advertising as a practice.[8] It would not be until much later in the century that the attention either of advertisers themselves or the government turned to any significant regulation of posters' content. Indeed, the only legal constraints specifically concerning the content of outdoor advertisements before 1889 were in the *Betting Acts* of 1853 and 1874 and the various pieces of legislation governing elections.[9]

What first attracted the attention of legislators was the capacity of outdoor advertising to be a material nuisance in urban spaces, reflecting something of the character and priorities of urban government of the time. Indeed, poster advertising's distinctly physical presence had not gone unnoticed by contemporary commentators. As Charles Dickens noted in 1851, posters were plastered so thickly on one building that the:

> ...crumpled remnants of old bills torn down, rotted away in wasting heaps of fallen leaves. Here and there, some of the thick rind of the house had peeled off in strips, and fluttered heavily down, littering the street; but, still, below these rents and gashes, layers of decomposing posters showed themselves, as if they were interminable. I thought the building could never even be pulled down, but in one adhesive heap of rottenness and poster.[10]

For Dickens, the sheer volume of posters meant that they had a physical existence beyond their brief lives as a message. The poster had become enmeshed with the fabric of the building and adjacent street, forming part of both the physical structure and viscerally material degradation of the Victorian city itself. Posters were certainly a nuisance to Dickens for the message they had the potential to carry, but here they were also a discernibly physical problem at a moment when those who governed cities were growing sensitive to the hygiene and material conditions of the urban environment.

[8] James Dawson Burn, *The Language of the Walls: And a Voice from the Shop Windows, or, the Mirror of Commercial Roguery* (London, 1855).

[9] *Betting Act*, 1853 (16 and 17 Vict. c. 119), s. 7; 1874 (37 and 38 Vict. c. 15), s. 9; *Corrupt and Illegal Practices Prevention Act*, 1883 (46 and 47 Vict. c. 212), s. 9(2) and 18; *Municipal Election (Corrupt and Illegal Practices) Act*, 1884 (47 and 48 Vict. c. 70), s. 4, 6 and 14.

[10] Charles Dickens, 'Bill Stickers', *Household Worlds*, 22 March 1851, reprinted in *The Complete Works of Charles Dickens: Reprinted Pieces, Vol. III* (New York, 2009), p. 112.

The issues caused by advertising were, by the middle-years of the century, beginning to be discussed in terms of dirt, detritus, property damage and obstruction. Indeed, the physical aspect of the outdoor advertisement was far more profound when applied to methods other than postering. In German writer Max Schlesinger's 1853 account of his 'saunterings' about London, he remarked upon the multitude of different methods and locations in which advertising might be found:

> The advertisement is omnipresent. It is in the skies and on the ground; it swells as the flag in the breeze, and it sets its seal on the pavement; it is on the water, on the steam-boat wharf, and under the water in the Thames tunnel; it roosts on the highest chimneys; it sparkles in coloured letters on street lamps...There is no escaping from the advertisement, for it travels with you in the omnibuses, in the railway carriages, and on the paddle-boxes of the steamers.[11]

As Thomas Richards observes the indistinguishability of the individual poster amongst the vast accretion of overlapping messages—presented memorably in John Orlando Parry's 1834 painting *A London Street Scene* (Fig. 2.1)—meant that sometime in the 1830s advertisers hit upon the idea of extending adverts to the streets themselves.[12]

Advertisers had for some time employed sandwich men, carrying a slogan on each side of a board slung over the shoulders, but horse-drawn vans typically bearing slogans on each side and often accompanied by a crier were an increasingly common sight on the streets of towns and cities during the 1830s. Indeed, vehicles shaped like oversized hats, boots and wigs were already in use by 1836, when the 'Delicate Advertisement Company' ('delicate' for their focus on messages aimed at those in 'pecuniary distress', not for their methods) advertised the forthcoming availability of 'ambulating scaffolds...varying from 40ft. to 80ft. long by 30ft. high', to display messages in 12-inch-high letters.[13] Describing the typical scene in the period some twenty years later, one journalist remembered:

[11] Max Schlesinger, *Saunterings In and About London* (London, 1853), pp. 40–41.

[12] Thomas Richards, *The Commodity Culture of Victorian England: Advertising and Spectacle, 1851–1914* (Stanford, 1990), pp. 45–48; see also: Richard Stein, *In Victoria's Year: English Literature and Culture, 1837* (Oxford 1996), pp. 45–46.

[13] *Saint James's Chronicle*, 5 May 1836, p. 4.

Fig. 2.1 John Orlando Parry, 'A London Street Scene' 1835 (*Source* The Alfred Dunhill Collection)

> Processions of boardmen to the extent of 200 or 300 frequently paraded London streets...Bands of music, in gaudy vans, perambulated the road, flanked on each side by rows of men bearing what was termed "a back and belly board" each. The procession was led by some fellow in a grotesque dress, and closed by one in equally ridiculous costume. An enormous bell, mounted on a van traversed London streets, and announced the advent of a paper called the Railway Bell.[14]

In his 1843 critique of British society *Past and Present*, polymath and essayist Thomas Carlyle cited the—now much reproduced by historians for its apparent era-defining absurdity—example of one advertising van shaped to resemble a seven-foot-tall hat.[15] In 1847, *Punch* imagined that, spurred-on by the rise of advertising inside omnibuses, advertising

[14] From the *Chatham News and North Kent Spectator*, reproduced in *Hertford Mercury and Reformer*, 15 December 1860, p. 4.

[15] Thomas Carlyle, *Past and Present* (London, 1843), p. 302.

vans of absurd size would soon be seen carrying passengers throughout London.[16]

Although much of Carlyle's ire was focused upon what he saw as an advertising strategy symptomatic of the questionable morality of commercial culture, his objection also highlighted the inescapably physical and spatially disruptive nature of advertising as a presence in the streets of the 1840s. Eight years later, Colonel Charles Sibthorp, the ultra-Tory MP for Lincoln, largely remembered for his fierce opposition to the Great Exhibition in the same year, proposed an unsuccessful bill to parliament which sought to ban 'advertising vans' and 'barrel organs' in the streets of London specifically for the nuisance they caused.[17] In April 1851, commending Colonel Sibthorp's crusade against 'the noisy invaders of public space and public safety' the barrel organ and the advertising van, the *Morning Post* judged that 'the enjoyment of Town-life is materially impeded by these abominable nuisances'.[18] In the same month, Marylebone vestry unanimously carried a motion that the 'Commissioners of Police take immediate steps for the abolition of the perambulating advertising van nuisance' arguing that 'many serious accidents had resulted from this nuisance' and unless measures were taken 'there was no doubt, in addition to the puffing tradesmen, the exhibitors of the suburban fairs and other places of amusement would adopt this mode of advertising to the great danger and inconvenience of the public'.[19] Debating the *Metropolitan Police Bill* with Sibthorp, Ross Donnelly Mangles, MP for Guildford, argued that 'the time had come when the Government ought to take some steps to remedy the evil' caused by advertising vans, following an incident where he was nearly unhorsed on Westminster Bridge.[20]

It would be easy to dismiss the views of Sibthorp, who maintained a parliamentary record of opposing any bill that had even a whiff of the twin evils of modernity or progress about it, as the knee-jerks of a man at odds with a rapidly changing world. Indeed, his views on outdoor

[16] *Punch*, 18 December 1847, p. 240.

[17] Sibthorp is also referred to as Sibthorpe. Hansard, House of Commons (HC) 16 June 1851, vol. 117, Column (cc) 790.

[18] *Morning Post*, 15 April 1851, p. 4.

[19] *Morning Advertiser*, 21 April 1851, p. 2.

[20] Hansard, HC, 12 June 1851, vol. 117, cc. 771.

advertising were lampooned by a cartoon in *Punch*—for whom he was a frequent target in their campaign against 'privilege, corruption and humbug'[21]—that depicted him in a boxing match against the adverting vans and on another occasion throwing himself beneath their wheels in despair.[22] However, the framing of his opposition to advertising vans for their obstruction of traffic flows and within the legal language of public nuisance was both contemporarily resonant and prescient of future conflicts. In 1853, what would become the *London Hackney Carriage Act* was introduced to parliament, garnering the opinion from Lord Stanley of Alderley—later notable as the first Muslim member of the House of Lords following his conversion to Islam—that its object was 'to put down the monster grievance of advertising vans, which at present encumbered the streets, and offered the greatest obstruction to the passage of the wayfarer'.[23] The final Act, passed into law shortly after, banned all advertising on the outside of vehicles, on horseback and even on foot that obstructed or annoyed inhabitants in London, and would, over the next fifty years, be incorporated as a feature of many of the provincial corporation and improvement acts discussed in the following chapters. Although challenging to enforce—sandwich men and the vagaries of the use of omnibuses for advertising would still periodically draw the ire of government for decades after[24]—in practice this meant that no vehicle could carry advertising except where they were delivering goods or on public transport, gradually bringing down the curtain on the brief era of the advertising van as public nuisance.[25]

Understanding forms of outdoor advertising as a very material nuisance (both in the general sense and in the more formal legal definition of

[21] Quoted in Richard D. Altick. *Punch: The Lively Youth of a British Institution, 1841–1851* (Columbus, 1997), p. xix.

[22] *Punch*, 10 May 1851, p. 189 and 28 June 1851, p. 6.

[23] Hansard, House of Lords (HL), 9 June 1853, vol. 127, cc. 1296.

[24] See, for example: Hansard, HC, 7 August 1862, vol. 168, cc. 1214.

[25] *London Hackney Carriage Act*, 1853 (16 and 17 Vict. ch. 33), s. 16.

'public nuisance'[26]) is central to grasping the impetus behind early opposition to it and the legislation that pushed outdoor advertisers towards the changes made in the 1860s. As legal historian Rachel Vorspan has shown in relation to prohibiting gatherings, nuisance proved to be a highly malleable concept that has been reinterpreted to suit the preoccupations of urban government since at least the start of the nineteenth century.[27] The earliest limits on outdoor advertising were not concerned with advertisements specifically, but were part of attempts to improve movement and remove unsightly, dirty or potentially dangerous obstructions in the increasingly crowded streets of eighteenth- and nineteenth-century cities. As early as 1762, the *London Streets Act* (amended many times thereafter), whilst centrally concerned with the maintenance of paving, stipulated that all signs that denoted the trade, occupation or calling of any person that encroached or projected into the street could be removed and reattached to houses and shops at the discretion of local commissioners.[28] In amongst the many provisions of the 1817 *Metropolitan Paving Act* were similar stipulations that hoardings, boards and scaffolding could not be erected without permission from the local commissioners or similar local authorisation.[29]

In their broadest senses, the 1762 and 1817 Acts sought specifically to improve the useability of and flows of traffic on the streets, but were hampered in their effectiveness by the complexities of local government and policing before the gradual changes of the later nineteenth century.[30] Indeed, the 1817 Act covered everything from the materials used for water pipes—decreasing the frequency of repairs to them—to controls on street traders and other undesirable persons and activities, the right

[26] Public nuisance is a common law offense that covers any act that 'endangers the life, health, morals or comfort of the public' or obstructs them 'in the exercise or enjoyment of rights common to all her Majesty's subjects' *Archbold's Criminal Pleading and Practice* (London, 1985) quoted in J.R. Spencer, 'Public NuisanceA Critical Examination', *Cambridge Law Journal* 48:1 (1989), pp. 55–84 (p. 55).

[27] Rachel Vorspan, 'Freedom of Assembly and the Right to Passage in Modern English Legal History', *San Diego Law Review* 921 (1997), pp. 927–1042.

[28] *London Streets Act*, 1762 (2 Geo. 3. c. 21); 1763 (3 Geo. 3. c. 23); 1764 (4 Geo. 3, c. 39); 1765 (5 Geo. 3, c. 50); and (6 Geo. 3, c. 54) and Larwood, *The History of Signboards*, pp. 28–29.

[29] *Metropolitan Paving Act*, 1817 (57 Geo. 3. c. 29), s. 75.

[30] Asa Briggs, *The Age of Improvement, 1783–1867* (London, 2014), p. 39.

for local authorities to compulsorily purchase obstructive private property, and an obligation for residents to shovel snow and ice from the pavements abutting their properties. Similar designs were evident in *The Towns Improvement Clauses Act* of 1847, which allowed local authorities to remove any signs or boards that projected into the streets in a manner that they saw as an obstruction, allowing for the levying of fines for non-compliance, and in the 1853 prohibition on advertising vans in the *Hackney Carriage Act*.[31]

Given this increasing focus on spatial order and regulation, it might be tempting to see patterns of outdoor advertising control by the mid-nineteenth century as part of an incipient practice of the forms of Joycean liberal governmentality that emerged in the latter part of the century.[32] However, a degree of caution is important here. The legislative objectives of the 1762 and 1817 acts and those that followed them were clothed in the ideology of 'improvement': the impulse to rational, gradual and piecemeal cumulative betterment that historians like Paul Slack and Asa Briggs showed emerging from the early-modern period and dominating urban reform into the nineteenth century.[33] Indeed, the acts that curtailed outdoor advertising were themselves part of the significant accumulation of *Improvement Acts* that were administered by local Improvement Commissioners.[34] Outdoor advertising was just one of many material nuisances that might obstruct the flows and functioning of cities because of the apparatus—boards, signs, vans and hoardings—that displayed it. Understanding advertising control here through the lens material nuisance, as Christopher Hamlin and David Churchill have shown with regard to municipal administration, public health and policing, tempers the urge to see a somewhat piecemeal form of spatial intervention as anything more than hinting at the programmatic forms

[31] *The Towns Improvement Clauses Act*, 1847 (10 and 11 Vict. c. 34), s. 69.

[32] Patrick Joyce, *The Rule of Freedom: Liberalism and the Modern City* (London, 2003); Chris Otter, 'Making Liberalism Durable: Vision and Civility in the Late Victorian City', *Social History* 27:1 (2002), pp. 1–15; Nikolas Rose, *Powers of Freedom: Reframing Political Thought* (Cambridge, 1999).

[33] Paul Slack, *The Invention of Improvement: Information and Material Progress in Seventeenth-Century England* (Oxford, 2015), p. 1; Briggs, *The Age of Improvement*.

[34] On Improvement Acts and Commissioners, see: Briggs, *The Age of Improvement*, p. 39.

of governmentality that emerged later in the century.[35] The legislation that dealt with advertising allowed authorities to deal with obstruction or public nuisance, but little consideration was yet given to the content and desirability of the advertisements beyond their material manifestation.

From around the 1840s onwards, though, new laws were emerging that targeted forms of outdoor advertising in a more specific manner. These new laws were essentially prohibitive, criminalising billposters and placing the onus on them to seek permission from property owners. The 1839 *Metropolitan Police Act*, which criminalised billposting without consent and the 1862 *Metropolitan Management Act Amendment*, which introduced penalties for sticking bills on lampposts, for example, created a legal framework that positioned posters as a disordered rather than obstructive presence, whilst also protecting property owners' rights.[36] Although still concerned with the physical nuisance that Dickens had identified, these pieces of legislation moved the discussion about posters beyond the more obviously physical aspect of nuisance and into more complex notions of regulation and control of public spaces. The middle of the century, then, was a period when a more piecemeal form of spatial intervention began to be married with a more holistic and recognisably regulatory framework for urban governance that, as the following section shows, was rooted in incorporating advertising as a civilised and ordered part of cities managed by local authorities.

In 1844, Manchester's recently minted Corporation exemplified how approaches to outdoor advertising were developing, banning the posting of bills without the property owner's consent, whilst also prohibiting the carrying of signs, boards and placards that caused obstruction.[37] In addition, section 60 of the Manchester act, in common with the *Towns Improvement Clauses Act* of 1847, allowed for the removal of signs and hoardings that overhung or obstructed streets and the imposition of fines

[35] David Churchill, *Crime Control and Everyday Life in the Victorian City: The Police and the Public* (Oxford, 2017); Christopher Hamlin, 'Nuisances and Community in Mid-Victorian England: The Attractions of Inspection', *Social History* 38:3 (2013), pp. 346–379.

[36] *Metropolitan Police Act*, 1839 (2 and 3 Vict. c. 47), s. 54 (10); *Metropolis Management Amendment Act*, 1862 (25 and 26 Vict. c. 102), s. 93.

[37] *Act for the Good Government and Police Regulation of the Borough of Manchester*, 1844 (7 and 8 Vict. c. 40), s. 60, 102 and 282.

against those who failed to comply.[38] Nevertheless, the way that advertising was opposed, at least in terms of legislation, was for its deleterious effects in places that it should not be, not because of its commercial nature or message. In contrast, as later chapters show, towards the end of the century, criticism of advertising would reposition it as inherently vulgar or damaging to both rural and urban experience in ways that were barely detectable for much of the nineteenth century.

Civilising Outdoor Advertising

As a number of historians have commented, by the mid-nineteenth century, British cities, especially London, were reaching a crucial moment in the balance between lived space, order and commercialism. The early acts that controlled advertising were in character largely defensive in nature, though they fell under the banner of improvement, but as approaches to urban management and regulation developed, they became more detailed and constructive in nature. Historians like Thomas Richards and Lynda Nead have argued that whilst advertising was intrinsic to the emerging commercial cultures, its chaotic nature was antagonistic to the orderly flows of consumers and capital in the metropolis.[39] Reducing obstructions caused by advertising hoardings, boards and vans was one way that these flows might be improved, but the process of creating greater order in advertising was also about creating a greater degree of order in how and where advertising was encountered. As Sarah Thornton, in common with Nead and Richards, argues, from the early 1850s, projects of modernisation and improvement focused upon the visual experience of London alongside the creation of smooth flows of people and traffic.[40] The Victorians were not uncomfortable with the idea of space being commercialised: rather, they were uncomfortable with the types of uncivilised capitalism represented by advertising in the early part of the century. Against this backdrop, the remaining years of the nineteenth

[38] *The Towns Improvement Clauses Act*, 1847 (10 and 11 Vict. c. 34), s. 69.

[39] Lynda Nead, *Victorian Babylon* (London, 2000); Richards, *The Commodity Culture of Victorian England*.

[40] Sara Thornton, *Advertising, Subjectivity and the Nineteenth-Century Novel Dickens, Balzac and the Language of the Walls* (London, 2009), pp. 4–7.

century saw both attempts by the state and by advertisers to alter the practices of outdoor advertising that shaped how outdoor advertising would be practised for the next century.

Indeed, the attempt to regulate outdoor advertising represented in the 1839 *Metropolitan Police Act* and later provisions in provincial towns and cities that banned posters without the property owner's permission were pursued rigorously from the 1840s. Notably, the police actively began to take action against bill stickers. In May 1841, a bill sticker named John Speechley, having been arrested for plastering the shutters of an empty house with his posters defended his 'right' as a 'free-born Englishman…to stick bills where I like'.[41] Confronted by the magistrate with the fact that he 'had no right to stick bills on people's houses', he responded that there was no 'notice to "stick no bills", so I'd a right to exercise the privileges of our profession'. Unsurprisingly, this contrary reading of the law found little favour. In November 1845, the police arrested and fined a William Burgess for posting the largest bill either the constable or the bill sticker himself had ever seen, consisting of 170 sheets, with three-foot-long letters advertising concerts in Covent Garden organised by the French conductor and composer Louis-Antoine Jullien.[42]

Against a background of greater scrutiny from the police and courts, the disordered and competitive nature of illegal bill sticking was of growing concern to the both the advertising industry and their customers. There was, aside from issues of postering itself, a great deal of bad publicity surrounding the fractious rivalries that arose between bill stickers. In Bristol in 1850, for example, two men were fined and imprisoned for seven days after they assaulted a rival bill sticker, defacing his posters and breaking a pasting brush over his head.[43] In September 1857, the *Leeds Mercury* reported that Samuel Leeming, who had been convicted of defacing others' bills, was charged with threatening assault on the competitor whose posters he had covered.[44] In Brighton in 1860, under the heading 'Two of a Trade Can Never Agree', it was reported that two men were arrested for defacing a rival billposters' rented site. The judge admonished both bill sticking companies for the results of their

[41] *The Northern Star*, 29 May 1841, p. 12.

[42] *London Evening Standard*, 25 November 1845, p. 4.

[43] *Bristol Times and Mirror*, 17 August 1850, p. 6.

[44] *Leeds Mercury*, 24 September 1857, p. 3.

rivalry, remarking that it was 'disgraceful to have two parties in the town thus conducting themselves'.[45] Whilst passing judgement at the Borough Police Court in Wolverhampton, F. Walton presiding not only fined the defendants for covering others' bills on a rented wall, but also suggested that 'it was wrong that through the quarrels of bill stickers the interests of their clients should be damaged'.[46]

Newspapers' criticism of bill stickers perhaps needs to be taken with a pinch of caution—the press were, after all, both customers of bill stickers and also their most direct competitors for advertisers' custom—nevertheless, their coverage is suggestive of customers becoming frustrated with the competition in the poster industry. In the *Leicester Chronicle* in September 1852, reporting on another case involving conflict between bill stickers over the defacement of bills, the editor appended the article, stating: 'we have also to complain of the erasure of our bills announcing the contents of the Chronicle and the removal of them from shops where they have been allowed to be placed'.[47] In October 1852, the *Alloa Advertiser* issued its own warning to bill stickers:

> Our readers do not require to be informed that there is a rivalry amongst bill-stickers...But this bill-sticking rivalry has just about arrived at an intolerable height... in performing the work [the bill-sticker's] contempt for the bills which may have been stuck up by any "brother in the trade" leads him most maliciously to cover these up and he in turn has his subjected to the same treatment by the first knight of the paste brush who goes around the district. Only the other morning, we detected one of these gentlemen with the placards of some universal medicine man in his possession, deliberately covering up freshly pasted bills, the property of merchants in Town. The Procurator-Fiscal has been made aware of this and an example will assuredly be made of the first bill sticker who wantonly defaces and destroys bills.[48]

Perhaps as a result of the often violent competition for advertising space, the more far-sighted advertising companies were increasingly moving towards renting specific sites and hoardings, letting them to customers and often retaining bill stickers to do the work for them. Married with

[45] *Brighton Gazette*, 29 November 1860, p. 6.

[46] *Wolverhampton Chronicle and Staffordshire Advertiser*, 24 November 1858, p. 4.

[47] *Leicester Chronicle*, 11 September 1852, p. 3.

[48] *Alloa Advertiser*, 30 October 1852, p. 3.

the laws restricting the posting of bills without permission, renting sites ensured a degree of exclusivity for customers and promised some legal remedy when posters were defaced. Founded in 1851, the London-based Metropolitan Permanent Advertising Company was one example that by 1859 offered 140 permanent advertising stations. These were typically located on street corners, railway stations or steamboat piers, and could display posters of at least seven feet six inches by three feet six inches whilst commanding a total rent of around £37 per month.[49] In 1855, W.H. Smith, expanding beyond the confines of its news-stands, signed a contract with the Chester and Holyhead Railway Company to be the sole contractor for all advertisements displayed in its stations.[50]

It's not clear exactly when these types of rented site became popular, but the evidence of prosecutions shows that from the 1840s there was significant friction between older postering companies or individual bill stickers and those that sought to rent or even purchase sites for their exclusive use. In June 1840, just months after the 1839 *Metropolitan Police Act*'s prohibitive powers came into force, five men, 'all knights of the paste-can', were charged with unlawfully posting upon and defacing hoardings rented to a billposting company surrounding Nelson's Column. This was, as the writer pointed out, a clash between rival approaches to billpostering, where the defendants were 'determined to stick up for their rights by sticking their bills over "the company's" hoarding'. Mr Scott, who employed the defendants, 'scorn[ed]' the process of renting hoardings for exclusive use, asserting that he postered 'in the old regular manner'.[51] One of the defendants, Thomas Mason, offered the following reason behind his actions, reproduced by the reporter with the characteristically heavy-handed approximation of the local dialect:

> I for one 'as summat to say; here is us hard-working men robbed of our living by a company, Lord! Who'd 'a thought a year or two ago of a Bill Sticking Company; but hang me if they don't company everything... Man and boy for nearly forty years I've stuck bills up agin every hoarding in London, and I never heard of one being private property.

[49] *The Globe*, 15 January 1859, p. 3; *Morning Chronicle*, 17 January 1859, p. 7.

[50] Terry Nevett, *Advertising in Britain: A History* (London, 1982), p. 122.

[51] *Morning Post*, 13 June 1840, p. 7.

As the *Morning Post* further suggested, the moves towards rented sites portended the 'annihilation of the independent body of bill stickers' by creating circumstances for the further criminalisation of traditional bill sticking, but also by creating a dichotomy between the civilised, ordered and legal sites for posters and the old-fashioned, disordered and independent bill stickers.[52]

In similar circumstances in January 1845, Patrick Lee, a bill sticker who styled himself the 'literary bill sticker for every publication in London', bemoaned the rise of the advertising station when was brought before magistrates for defacing sites owned by a Mr Quinn[53] In August 1857, Joseph Lucock was fined 10 shillings for posting on a noticeboard at King's Cross that was the property of the Metropolitan Advertising Company, again for covering others' bills.[54] Such was the reduction in acts of defacement, that by 1858 a column in *The Builder*, ostensibly decrying the poor quality of poster art, argued that:

> A marked improvement has however taken place…since the plan has been adopted of establishing permanent advertising stations in suitable and prominent situation. Before this the rivalry of bill stickers caused even the largest and most elaborate handbills, if they may be so called, to be rapidly defaced.[55]

The close policing of these advertising stations too seems to have become a known fact of daily life by this period. In 1866, in an interview with one John Smith, who scraped together a meagre living scavenging and selling waste paper, the subject told the *London City Mission Magazine* that 'I tears the bills off the walls when I get a chance - not at the advertising stations, Sir; Oh dear no…That 'ud be a month if they caught you at and it ain't worth the risk'.[56] Though the veracity of the interview might be questionable, the content serves to illustrate just how effectively the

[52] Ibid.

[53] *Lloyds Weekly Newspaper*, 19 January 1845, p. 4. This is the earliest use this author could find of the specific terminology 'advertising stations' clarified here as meaning 'The front or side walls of houses in commanding situations throughout the metropolis on which boards with painted frames are placed for the reception of placards'.

[54] *The Morning Advertiser*, 1 August 1857, p. 7.

[55] *The Builder*, 30 October 1858, vol. 16. p. 722.

[56] *London City Mission Magazine*, 1 May 1866, vol. 31, p. 99.

distinction between legitimately posted advertising and now-illegal bill sticking had been absorbed into popular discourse.

Nor were these changes restricted to the capital, either. In Leeds, the growing trend was apparent in a series of posters produced by Edward Sheldon, who's supposed centrality to reform in the business of outdoor advertising opened this chapter, posted around the city in 1862. They stated that Sheldon, Son and Co. had provided a series of advertising station across the city which they claimed would 'protect the interests common to themselves and their patrons' adding that 'numerous notices "stick no bills" were being rapidly multiplied and the places available were becoming so circumscribed that there was not the necessary convenience remaining to ensure publicity'.[57] In a swipe at the continuing hostility from independent bill stickers and local competitors, they added that they were 'aware that certain persons, whose interest it is to misrepresent our conduct have done all in their power to impugn our motives and to injure our character, to which we have one simple answer: in a town like Leeds there is ample room for all' adding that accusations that they were forming a monopoly were mere 'silly talk'. Indeed, Sheldon's assertion appears to have been true: in 1865, rival advertising company Wood and Holdsworth claimed 'first-class advertising stations in all the principal throughfares' in Leeds, whilst Clayton and Son of nearby Bradford advertised similar advertising stations in Leeds newspapers throughout 1866.[58]

From the 1840s onwards and notably from the middle of the 1860s, advertising companies were taking advantage of the way laws were framed, the emphasis placed by the state on nuisances and order, and their ability to rent hoardings in prominent, typically unused locations to establish a monopoly on legitimate advertising space. Evidence suggests that the various railway companies were around this time becoming keen on realising the potential value of renting out their property, which usually had heavy footfall and advantageous locations. In addition to W.H. Smith's contracts for railway hoardings, in 1857 the Great North of Scotland Railway Company invited advertisers to rent space at their stations, and in 1871, Glasgow and South Western Railways invited offers in trade

[57] The poster is reproduced in: Nelson and Sykes, *Outdoor Advertising*, p. 10.

[58] Unknown Author, *Tommy Toddless Comic Almenac* (sic) (Leeds, 1865), p. 10; *Leeds Mercury*, various, but see, for example, 18 June 1866, p. 4.

journals for the exclusive rights to display advertisements on all of their stations.[59] Moreover builders, who were often required by law to place hoardings around construction and demolition sites for public safety, latched on to the ability to rent out these hoardings as a lucrative source of income, which went unchallenged in law until 1889 and the *Advertising Stations (Ratings) Act*.[60]

Of course, though Edward Sheldon and his contemporaries may have claimed they sought no monopoly, their motivations were squarely aimed at cornering as much of the market in their local areas as possible. Sheldon's company boasted that by 1876 it had over 500 advertising stations around Leeds and Bradford and by the 1880s regional newspapers in everywhere from Glasgow to Shepton Mallet featured regular advertisements from billposting companies who claimed to command the best and most numerous advertising stations in the locale.[61] The other strategies by which they sought to establish greater control of the industry were through the establishment of billposter's associations. Various associations were established at around the same time and the two most successful continued to compete with each other until they amalgamated at the beginning of the 1890s.[62] There is much that could be said about the activities of the associations, but the salient element here was the production and distribution of trade directories that listed 'approved' billposters who were members of the association in the local area. The directories offered potential customers a supposedly reliable and reputable billposter, who would not engage in the unseemlier activities of the independent bill stickers.

The United Kingdom Billposters Association (UKBPA)—which after considerable wrangling seems to have emerged as the dominant association outside London—of which Edward Sheldon was a founding member, also stipulated that only limited numbers of advertising companies would be included in the directory for each town. One member for a town with a population under 50,000, two for towns of between 50,000 and 150,000, three up to 300,000 and four up to 400,000, with separate

59 *Aberdeen Herald and General Advertiser*, 31 January 1857, p. 4; *Railway News and Joint Stock Journal*, 25 February 1871, vol. 15, no. 374, p. 1.

60 See Chapter 5.

61 *Yorkshire and Leeds Intelligencer*, 20 January 1876, p. 1.

62 Sheldon, *History of Poster Advertising*, p. 20.

rules for London, which was largely covered by the independent London Poster Advertising Association.[63] Accordingly, in the 1860s, poster advertising companies began to declare their affiliation as members of the UKBPA or similar in their newspaper advertisements.[64] Although conflict between members and rival associations continued, the billposting associations enforced strict standards of behaviour, fixed prices for certain jobs in local areas and in later years, allowed for a degree of political advocacy on behalf of their members. However, the importance of their role in their first decades was to contribute to the consolidation of the industry and its practices, monopolising advertising space in towns and cities and gradually eroding the presence of independent billposters. As Cyril Sheldon demonstrated, the principal result of the associations and their directories was consolidation. In 1879, the directory of the UKBPA listed 406 names covering 376 towns, with a high point in 1885 of 522. Yet by 1937 only 338 names coved 1,121 towns plus London, whilst a dozen of these firms controlled the bulk of the advertising space in the country.[65]

The advertising station thus represented the bringing of a degree of order to what had been a disordered and often disreputable practice, but it was merely the simplest of these more ordered forms of outdoor advertisement. In his 1863 book *Advertise, How? When? Where?* William Smith argued that the advertising industry had failed to follow the cues that the 1851 Great Exhibition had provided, by realising the potential of advertising as a public 'spectacle'.[66] Smith was perhaps too harsh—the commercial importance of the advertising station was perhaps the defining innovation of the period, mundane though it now seems—in reality outdoor advertisers were already alert to the possibilities of technological advances and innovative platforms for their posters and signs. In 1851, for example, the Metropolitan Sanitary and Convenience Advertising Company was formed—although failing soon after—not only to remedy a claimed deficiency in the provision of 'public water-closets and urinals', but also to 'afford a ready means of extensively advertising at

[63] Sheldon, *History of Poster Advertising*, p. 7.

[64] *Sheffield Daily Telegraph*, 5 February 1857, p. 2; *Loughborough Monitor*, 8 February 1866, p. 4; *Bradford Daily Telegraph*, 15 November 1866, p. 2 for three of many examples.

[65] Sheldon, *History of Poster Advertising*, p. 11.

[66] Richard, *The Commodity Culture of Victorian England*, passim, but here at p. 21, William Smith, *Advertise, How? When? Where?* (London, 1863), p. 14.

a low cost'.[67] As illumination became a possibility towards the end of the decade, several companies erected pillars covered in advertising that contained clocks or information about travelling distances to give a sheen of usefulness, whilst some enterprising advertisers, including the Permanent Advertising Company, made use of painted and stained glass in street lamps hired from the local authorities.[68] In 1859, the vestry of St George-the-Martyr rented all its available lampposts at £1 each for the display of advertising.[69] Although some local authorities received the offer of 20 shillings (later raised to £2, then further to three guineas) per lamp post with some enthusiasm, they were opposed by retailers who disliked the idea of illuminated advertisements in close proximity to their premises and by editorial comment that questioned the benefits to the public.[70] Despite objections, the creation of the four-sided glass advertising boxes on street lamps became a common feature in both London and the provinces, although they were notably rejected by Liverpool, hinting at the ambivalence of the city to advertising over the next century.[71] As Lynda Nead has shown, though sometimes controversial, illumination behind shop windows was central to the spectacle of consumption being created in the metropolis and by adapting street lamps, advertising companies were inserting themselves into the fabric of towns in a more materially permanent, civilised and ordered way than they had before.[72]

These attempts to accommodate advertising space within the law and in concert with local government were, however, not always enthusiastically received. In 1859, MP William Cowper, returning to the idea of public nuisance, unsuccessfully introduced a bill to extend the provisions of the *Metropolitan Police Act* for the prevention of obstructions from advertisements on London's streets, aimed squarely at the illuminated

[67] *Morning Advertiser*, 10 July 1851, p. 1.

[68] *Rochdale Observer*, 13 August 1859, p. 2; *Morning Advertiser*, 27 October 1859.

[69] *Lambeth and Southwark Advertiser*, 9 July 1859, p. 2.

[70] *The Era*, 30 October 1859, p. 9 and *Holborn Journal*, 4 November 1859 ran the same column objecting to the proposals and referred to the idea as 'vandalism'. Also, *Lincolnshire Chronicle*, 23 December 1859, p. 7 quoting *The Times*. On the improved offers *Marylebone Mercury*, 26 November 1859, p. 3 and 21 January 1860, p. 4.

[71] *Liverpool Mail*, 14 April 1860, p. 6, see also Chapter 5.

[72] Nead, *Victorian Babylon*, p. 70.

pillars and street light enclosures.[73] He argued that these purpose-built structures that resembled a 'Chinese pagoda or and immense piece of confectionary' caused 'nuisance' and 'obstruction' despite their claims to be public information points. Indeed, he received support from the local press who, despite congratulating local government on their financial acumen in renting space to advertisers, argued that their city was being 'converted into an immense advertising station ...and that all the bill stickers and tenth-rate artists in London had been permanently engaged (under the immediate superintendence of the vestry) for this disfigurement of the principal street'. They continued that 'every blank wall or open space has become the station for advertisements more or less "permanent" and our places of public resort such as pleasure gardens, music halls and railway stations are made subservient to the bill sticker'.[74]

Indeed, the problem for opponents of structures produced specifically for advertising like Cowper was that suitable legislation for their regulation already existed. The 1855 *Metropolis Local Management Act* had made it unlawful for anyone to erect a hoarding or scaffold for any purpose without a licence from the local authority, whilst similar acts would follow in the provinces.[75] The effect of these acts was to strengthen the relationship between civilised forms of commodity culture and local authorities' capacity to regulate the urban spaces, and subsequent changes deepened this relationship. *The Metropolis Management Amendment Act*, 1862, confirmed that it was prohibited to post bills on lampposts or public buildings, whilst the *Metropolitan Streets Act 1867* prevented the carrying or distribution of advertising within six miles of Charring Cross without permission from the police. What prevented a reduction in outdoor advertisements was not the legal situation, but rather that the judgement rested in the hands of local vestries and corporations, who, at this stage, still showed very little dislike for advertisements unless they caused physical nuisance. Indeed, where they could use unoccupied public space to augment rates, many local authorities were eager to take advertisers' money.

[73] Hansard, HC, 1 August 1859, vol. 155, cc. 838.

[74] *Lambeth and Southwark Advertiser*, 9 July 1859, p. 2.

[75] *Metropolis Local Management Act*, 1855 (18 and 19 Vict. c. 120), s. 122 and 123. Acts outside of London are discussed in Chapter 3 in more detail.

There is also little evidence that there was yet any great popular objection to advertising as a practice in itself. By 1861, a correspondent to the *Suffolk and Essex Free Press*, calling themselves only 'Ventilate', declared:

> The present is essentially an advertising age... [in the metropolis] we find every available inch of blank space converted into a veritable Californian placer under the Midas-like touch of an "Advertising Company." Dead walls burst into vigorous and productive life; "hoardings" enable their fortunate owners to add to their hoards; the end of a house is the beginning of a fortune; and premises near a station alter a man's station in life astonishingly. Artistically decorated and illuminated columns, railway carriages, omnibuses, cabs, windows, bars, parlours, proclaim to the compelled observer where every want from bed and breakfast to the Polish for his boots must be readily, satisfactorily, and economically obtained.[76]

Although Ventilate did, unsurprisingly for a newspaper, go on to extol the even greater virtues of advertising in the press, they encapsulated the tone of attitudes to advertising: that it was a ubiquitous, almost symbolic aspect of the modern city.

Although there were voices that objected, most commentators seem to have been at worst ambivalent to outdoor advertising, if only occasionally enthusiastic. As Terry Nevett has argued, in this period objections to advertising from the general public appear to have been fairly sparse with music-hall songs of the 1860s reflecting a certain amusement at the increasing proliferation of posters, but little antipathy.[77] Advertising was part of what Richardson and Nead identified as the spectacle of modern, urban life and, in the middle-years of the nineteenth century, it was often framed as such. Over Christmas 1863 in the regular 'London Sayings and Doings' column that ran, amongst other locations, in the *Wrexham Advertiser*, the correspondent depicted spectacular displays of advertising as one of the thrilling aspects of London's seasonal festivities:

> The theatres are making most extensive preparations for "boxing night" and the immense placards upon the "advertising stations" and walls announcing the various pantomimes are wonderful specimens of the art

[76] *Suffolk and Essex Free Press*, 21 February 1861, p. 4.

[77] H.J. Waymark 'Advertising', 1865, quoted by Terry Nevett, *Advertising in Britain: A History* (London, 1982), p. 119.

> of printing as well as of posting. All this outlay - and it is a very considerable - amply repays itself, for the crowds that rushed to every place of public amusement… is something to be wondered at.[78]

A year later, another correspondent commented that they had seen plans that would 'eclipse' all of the current forms of advertising. These consisted of 'revolving advertising stations; and to make these attractive an automaton trumpeter should be placed in the centre of each who should jump like a Jack in the box in the air and commence sounding his instrument three times a day'.[79] Although this innovation does not seem to have come to fruition, it captures some of both the acceptance of advertising and its broad integration as part of the emerging urban spectacle. As the next chapter shows, it was the ubiquitous nature of advertising that would eventually lead to the first challenges to its visual primacy in the urban landscape. Yet before the 1870s, there is little evidence of any significant backlash.

Conclusion

The success of advertising companies and local government, if it might be termed so, was that since the beginning of the nineteenth century they had thrashed out something of an accommodation between the rapidly accelerating commercial culture, of which advertising was a key element, and the functioning of urban space. As the willingness of local government to allow outdoor advertising to embed itself within the fabric of towns and cities showed, especially where rents bolstered their rates, there was little tension between commercial and public space, so long as advertising was ordered and unobstructive. Commentators like Carlyle or John Ruskin and H.G. Wells might have decried the 'invasive aesthetics of advertised spectacle' and resisted the call of advertising 'puffery' for the moral degradation they saw in it, but local government and the public seemed to have little concern about this avowedly commercial presence.[80] For the time being, the central notion that governed outdoor advertising was simply that it should not cause public nuisance nor restrict the

[78] *Wrexham Advertiser*, 26 December 1863, p. 6.

[79] *Teesdale Mercury*, 2 November 1864, p. 6.

[80] Richards, *The Commodity Culture of Victorian England*, p. 255.

physical flows of crowded cities, that it should not provoke disorder nor cause more mess than was necessary. Nevertheless, the more far-sighted and entrepreneurial billposters seem to have recognised that there was little long-term tolerance for the disordered and uncivilised billposting and advertising practices that had raised the ire of commentators and legislators alike. It would take many decades, but through the creation of advertising stations, the consolidation of the industry and the slow elimination of the independent bill sticker, they gradually cornered the market and brought a more ordered and regulated approach to outdoor advertising.

In 1871, *The Clerkenwell News*, seeking advertising space for itself, ran a request for 'advertising stations...in all parts of London and the Suburbs, in conspicuous places where the advertisements and News can be read without causing obstruction to the public thoroughfare'.[81] The stipulation that the advertisements should not cause obstruction acknowledged the uncivilised nature of advertising vans and sandwich men, and the emphasis on finding specific advertising stations betokened the 'civilising' of the industry's practices that meant the newspaper no longer considered simply handing a pile of bills to a contractor to be effective advertising practice. For the moment, the accommodation between advertisers and the local state remained primarily about defining a set of spatial rules about how it should be conducted and how intrusive it might be in a physical sense. Indeed, by the final decades of the century, there is evidence that local corporations were actively seeking advertisers' money. In 1871, for example, Bristol's Local Board of Health advertised for bids to let 'the lamp-posts of the city for advertising stations, and hiring out he horizontal bar as a pendant for little boards'.[82] This situation, however, did not last. As the next chapter demonstrates, the seemingly endless appropriation of the visual environment of the 'advertising age' that 'Ventilate' had described in 1861 was by the end of the 1880s being opposed by emerging views on how lived spaces should be used, governed and experienced, whilst local corporations had begun to show an ever-more detailed and comprehensive interest in possessing the statutory tools to regulate urban space.

[81] *Clerkenwell News*, 20 January 1871, p. 1.

[82] *Devizes and Wiltshire Gazette*, 5 September 1872, p. 3.

CHAPTER 3

Opposition Emerges

Abstract This chapter looks at the development of opposition to outdoor advertising from around the 1870s that betokens a fledgling set of ideas about what lived space was for and how the experience of it should be regulated. It illustrates the emergence of two strands of opposition: the first strand of was from local government, who were expanding attempts to regulate and control the urban environment in ever more detailed ways. Outdoor advertising control thus fits into broader patterns of improvement, inspection and regulation that characterised local government in the later nineteenth century. The second strand came from those who felt that outdoor advertising was a disruptive presence in the urban setting in ways that went beyond physical nuisance. Advertising was presented as a disfiguring beautiful and historic architecture, its content and influence on public morals were questioned, and its interference with the well-being of the population started to raise concerns amongst a small band of influential groups.

Keywords Improvement · Local government · Sky signs · Governmentality · Morality · Censorship

J. Greenhalgh, *Injurious Vistas: The Control of Outdoor Advertising, Governance and the Shaping of Urban Experience in Britain, 1817–1962*, Palgrave Studies in Economic History,
https://doi.org/10.1007/978-3-030-79018-9_3

The irony of the way that the outdoor advertising industry had begun to consolidate and order its practices throughout the middle and later years of the nineteenth century was perhaps that by organising so effectively, it ultimately made itself a more easily tackled target for control than the unfettered billposting industry would likely ever have been. The nature of the business—tending towards ever greater and more spectacular displays that pushed the limits of the available space and technology, attracting the attention of those who objected on aesthetic grounds—meant outdoor advertising was framed from the 1870s onwards as a growing, damaging and uncontrollable presence in cities. As a result, in the final decades of the century, two related lines of opposition to outdoor advertising emerged. The first strand of opposition to emerge was from local government, who were expanding attempts to regulate and control the urban environment in ever more detailed ways. The second came from those who felt that outdoor advertising was a disruptive presence in the urban setting in ways that went beyond the physical nuisance of hoardings and vans. Advertising was presented as a disfiguring presence amongst beautiful and historic architecture, its content and influence on public morals were questioned, and its interference with the well-being of the population started to raise concerns amongst a small band of influential groups.

This chapter looks at the development of a more coherent discourse of opposition to outdoor advertising that emerged from around the 1870s and betokens a fledgling set of ideas about what lived space was for and how the experience of it should be regulated. I use 'lived space' here because towards the end of the century the debates over advertising control spilled beyond the urban and into the countryside, where, by the inter-war period, advocates of outdoor advertising control would enjoy their most satisfying successes. In stressing the development of approaches to lived space that considered how it might be made more functional, orderly and legible, the chapter suggests that outdoor advertising control fits into broader patterns of improvement, inspection and regulation that characterised the expansion of local government in the late nineteenth century.[1] Advertising control exposes discourses couched both

[1] Tom Crook, 'Sanitary Inspection and the Public Sphere in Late Victorian And Edwardian Britain: A Case Study in Liberal Governance', *Social History* 32:4 (2007), pp. 369–393.

in questions of obstruction and nuisance as well as how urban environments influenced public morality and helped or hindered the production of greater civility through governed spaces. The first section argues that a desire to exert greater potential control of the siting and rating of adverts was one of the many forms of mundane spatial intervention that demonstrates a more comprehensive approach to knowledge and regulation of urban space from the 1870s or so. Legislation from the 1870s onwards, particularly the emblematic *Public Health Act* of 1875, whilst aimed at squarely at preventing illness and poor health, also gave impetus to the creation of more intricate systems of spatial regulation like building regulations.[2] As, for example, Katrina Navickas and Bill Luckin have shown how regulating refuse and litter meant seeing what was in the streets differently; tackling streets 'caked in horse dung', for example, meant discovering new classifications and forms of filth and detritus to contain and eliminate.[3] Outdoor advertising is here just one of a host of problems that the state was beginning to 'see' as it turned a regulatory gaze to its streets. The chapter thus shows the emergence of a form of governance that was beginning to construe nuisance and disorder in terms that went beyond the physical.[4]

The second part of the chapter expands upon this idea, by examining the development of a discourse surrounding the nuisance of advertising as a less material, more visual element of the environment and the development of a discourse of public opposition to outdoor advertising. By the 1880s there was a small but influential cast of voices expressing concern over the content and effect of advertising on the experience of urban space and the general public, exemplified in calls for greater control and for censorship. In an era where grand infrastructural projects were bearing fruit, outdoor advertising was being increasingly contested as a disruptive element that reduced the benefits of planned civic display and infrastructural redevelopment. Objections couched in terms of architectural damage, the effect on the mental state of city dwellers and questions

[2] Michael F. James, *Construction Law* (London, 1994), pp. 63–64.

[3] Bill Luckin, 'Pollution in the City', in Martin Daunton (ed), *Cambridge Urban History of Britain, Vol. 3, 1840–1950* (Cambridge, 2000), pp. 207–228; Katrina Navickas, 'Keep Britain Tidy: From Public Health to Patriotism in the Twentieth-Century Campaign Against Litter', *Unpublished Paper*, 2021.

[4] Patrick Joyce, *The Rule of Freedom: Liberalism and the Modern City* (Manchester, 2003), p. 62.

of public decency here highlight the changing view of what urban space was for and the role it played in producing civilised citizens and society. Section three then examines the way that some more consistent forms of legislation on outdoor advertising were emerging in local government before ending with a discussion of sky signs. This builds on James Taylor's work to show how the control of sky signs in 1891 reveals the way discourses of advertising control were organising around questions of the effects of outdoor advertising as an aspect of urban experience. The exceptionality of the sky signs outcry towards the end of the century shows how embedded questions about the experience of the urban environment had become in public discourse, as well as revealing the expectations concerning the role of the state in managing that environment.

Hoardings, Rating and Local Government Control

As the previous chapter argued, the process of framing laws that dealt with outdoor advertising in the middle years of the nineteenth century led to a brief accord of sorts between local government and advertising companies. Illegal flyposting of bills would persist as a nuisance into the twentieth century, although they continually reduced as brand names sought only to deal with the 'respectable' billposting companies.[5] As long as advertising companies' activities remained ordered, caused no physical nuisance and avoided the chaos and, sometimes, violence, of the competition between bill stickers, the expansion of advertising stations to every wall, corner and hoarding was, for the most part, an accepted aspect of the commercial environment of the modern city. In this sense, the outdoor advertisement had a number of similarities to the shop window's emergence in the spectacle of Victorian commercial culture, but like the shop window the 1870s onwards signalled a period of greater scrutiny that reflected emerging anxieties over urban order and regulation centred on concerns over the experience and effect of urban space on the population.[6]

A factor in this general acceptance from local authorities before the 1870s was a certain view that the city was a functional commercial

[5] David Bernstein, *Advertising Outdoors: Watch This Space!* (London, 1997), p. 12; W. Hamish Fraser, *The Coming of the Mass Market, 1850–1914* (London, 1981), pp. 135–138.

[6] Lynda Nead, *Victorian Babylon* (London, 2000), pp. 149–206.

environment. Perhaps more importantly though, before the 1870s local government often lacked the capacity or the desire to involve itself in the kind of detailed governance of lived space that advertising control demanded.[7] Nevertheless the creation of laws that governed postering on public property in the middle of the century signalled a move towards a more vigilant regulatory approach. As John Davis has shown, from the 1870s until at least the 1890s central government made efforts to facilitate and even encourage municipal experimentation, by creating permissive legislation and allowing the expansion of local government's remit.[8] One of the first examples of a local body pushing for more comprehensive powers to control the siting of outdoor advertisements was the 1871 *Huddersfield Improvement Act*, under which the corporation could prevent anyone from posting an advertisement or bill without the corporation's consent, a level of control that would be requested, yet rarely attained by other authorities over the next seventy years.[9] The act also added powers to remove anything indecent or obscene, prefiguring the *Indecent Advertisements Act* by 18 years. Though considerably ahead of its time, the character of these sections of the Huddersfield act showed the corporation considering outdoor advertising as more than merely a material nuisance.

However, there is no sense these fledgling attempts at local regulation sought to eliminate outdoor advertising entirely. Though advertising companies and even parliament often assumed that local control would be a pathway to total suppression, it was not, for example, until the 1930s that similar powers garnered by the Chester Corporation in 1884 began to actually be exercised.[10] Twenty years after their act was passed Huddersfield Corporation still saw little issue with allowing advertising

[7] On the developing capacities and remit of local government see: James Chandler, *Explaining Local Government: Local Government in Britain Since 1800*, (Manchester, 2007), pp. 70–92; Barry M. Doyle, 'The Changing Functions of Urban Government: Councillors, Officials and Pressure Groups', in *The Cambridge Urban History of Britain, Vol. 3 1840–1950* (Cambridge, 2000), pp. 287–314.

[8] John Davis, 'Central Government and the Towns', in Martin Daunton (ed), *The Cambridge Urban History of Britain, Vol. 3 1840–1950* (Cambridge, 2000), pp. 261–286 (p. 263).

[9] *Huddersfield Improvement Act*, 1871 (34 and 35 Vict. c. 151), s. 71 and 232.

[10] Sheldon, *History of Poster Advertising*, p. 130.

on trams, from which they reputedly derived £3000 per year.[11] Though the London County Council (LCC) by the 1890s prohibited advertisements on hoardings connected to the council's works as a general rule, they were pragmatic enough to relax these restrictions when the financial incentive was sufficient, usually on land that was unused or presently deemed surplus.[12] In Manchester by 1895 the Corporation had resolved not to let any hoardings managed by the Improvements Committee for advertising, yet the Library Committee was quite willing to earn extra money by letting hoardings on their own sites.[13]

Local authorities' concerns appear to have been simply about having the *potential* to deal with the particular, local issues that occasionally arose in connection to advertising stations, particularly hoardings, a power that existing legislation did not provide. In 1870, for example, the Clerkenwell vestry in London heard from a deputation of tradesmen who complained that 'serious injury' was being done to their businesses by the presence of an advertising hoarding owned by the Metropolitan Railway Company. The hoarding surrounded a row of long-demolished houses, but due to the advantageous location in the city it was the opinion of both the business owners and the vestry that the railway company refused to develop the land as advertising space was a more lucrative source of rental revenue.[14] In Hackney too during the 1870s there were several attempts to establish precedent for the local authority to remove advertising hoardings, but in one case Chief Justice Cockburn confirmed that, as Clerkenwell had concluded, a local authority had no control over how hoardings were used once erected.[15] In St Pancras in 1875, complaints from residents in Albany Street over 'injury to their property' caused by 'the walls of the Colosseum being used as [an] advertising station' also contended that hoardings were being left up longer than necessary because of the considerable rental income generated by advertising sites.

[11] *Huddersfield Daily Examiner*, 19 September 1891, p. 13.

[12] For example, the LCC allowed advertising on hoardings enclosing surplus land, but left it up to the discretion of individual committees when dealing with council works. *The Times*, 8 July 1896, p. 6.

[13] *The British Architect*, 6 September 1895, p. 161.

[14] *Clerkenwell News*, 9 May 1870, p. 6.

[15] *Shoreditch Observer*, 6 October 1877, p. 3.

Although the chairman of the Works Committee did not doubt the 'great annoyance' caused, he confirmed that they had no powers to intervene.[16]

Unable to resolve these types of individual cases, in 1874 the Metropolitan Board of Works sought the legal powers to prohibit advertising where they saw fit. However, they were rebuffed by parliament on the grounds that it would be damaging to the poster industry.[17] Opponents in parliament maintained a position to which successive generations of advocates for the advertising industry would return, assuming that granting powers to local government would immediately mean complete suppression of the industry. MP for Truro James Hogg asserting that if 'bill sticking were prohibited, a large number of men, upon whom their wives and children were dependent for bread, would be thrown out of employment'.[18] Despite the general reticence of parliament to approve any laws that restricted commercial freedom, instances of advertising conflicting with other commercial interests—like those in Clerkenwell and St Pancras—were complicating any simple arguments concerned with restrictions on trade. Accordingly, a small number of corporations were able to make successful cases to expand their powers. Chester and Carlisle followed Huddersfield's example in 1884 and 1887, obtaining powers to create byelaws that allowed them to arbitrarily prohibit signs and advertisements in any location.[19] These types of laws remained relatively rare though, with local authorities more commonly sticking to the longer-term pattern of controlling obstructive advertising apparatus like scaffolding or vans, or making use of existing powers to restrict flyposting.

The issue of regulating hoardings was, however, gradually attracting enough attention that at the end of the 1880s parliament began to take an expansion of local powers seriously. Nevertheless, a change was only facilitated by pressure to consider how local authorities might tax rented advertising stations. The development of advertising stations as a common part of the urban furniture meant that there were difficulties over whether the owner of the property or the advertiser renting

[16] *Marylebone Mercury*, 2 October 1875, p. 2.

[17] Hansard, HC, 20 April 1874, vol. 218, cc. 1347 and 1356.

[18] Hansard, HC, 20 April 1874, vol. 218, cc. 1347.

[19] *Chester Improvement Act, 1884* (47 and 48 Vict. c. 239), s. 146; *Carlisle Corporation Act, 1887* (50 Vict. Sess. 2. c. 19), s. 147.

the billposting station was in possession or occupation of the hereditament and therefore liable to be rated. Against a background where rental income for advertising stations exceeded the rent an owner could expect from other uses, local authorities questioned whether advertising stations were rateable properties in their own right.[20] Between 1874 and 1877, for example, advertising contractor James Willing successfully battled the St Pancras Assessment Committee through the courts to establish that an advertisement station he had placed in the vacant garden of a house did not render him in occupation of the land for rating.[21] In the same period the Thorpe and Shaw advertising company in Manchester appealed successfully against a decision to rate their advertising hoardings in nearby Salford on the same grounds.[22] That the legal position still, however, needed clarification was illustrated in 1887 when the township of Pendleton, near Manchester, won their case against the Manchester Guardian Advertising Company who were deemed to be rateable for two plots on which they maintained advertising stations.[23]

The problems of rating advertising stations and broader questions of their control by local government had not excited much discussion before the 1870s, something that is indicative both of the consolidation of the advertising industry and the expanding and ever-more-detailed gaze of local authorities. Nevertheless, given the difficulties thrown-up by the series of court cases, by 1888 MP for Westminster William Burdett-Coutts' proposed an *Advertisement Rating Bill*, which was eventually passed late in 1889.[24] The *Advertising Stations (Rating) Act (ASRA)*, alongside the *Indecent Advertisement Act* (discussed shortly) mark-out 1889 as the year that concerns over outdoor advertising and their place in the urban environment began to be acknowledged at the level of national government. The *ASRA* created greater certainty about what might be rated—although it failed to adequately delineate the different parts of the

[20] See Chapter 2 on rental incomes from advertising and *The Graphic*, 11 February 1882, p. 6, for example, which reported that rental income for advertising was more than 15% higher than letting the land for other purposes.

[21] Edward Bullock, *The Law Journal Reports*, 1877 (London,1877), pp. 243–251.

[22] *Manchester Evening News*, 8 May 1876, p. 4.

[23] *Wigan Observer and District Advertiser*, 16 July 1887, p. 2.

[24] *Advertising Stations (Rating) Act*, 1889 (52 and 53 Vict. c. 27).

property, which led to continued difficulties until the 1948 *Local Government Act*[25]—but it also contained an equally important addition. Section five of the act allowed that, where a contractor was granted permission for a temporary hoarding, the local authority had the power to prohibit advertisements. Though this was a relatively minor piece of legislation, it is important here because it represents both an expansion of power and detailed regulation on the part of the local authorities, and a recognition by central government that governing urban environments involved some compromises over advertisers' commercial freedom.

Defining the Problem: Disfigurement, Experience and Obscenity

Advertising stations and hoarding were from the 1870s encountering the regulatory gaze of the local and central state in ways that unbalanced the brief period of largely unfettered use of the built environment for advertising. The hoarding and the poster were slowly entering a discursive space where, as well as being regulated by government as a potential physical nuisance, they were challenged as potentially disordering and disfiguring in ways that considered their impact upon the experience of urban, and later rural environments. It is little coincidence that this consideration of the effects of public space upon the citizenry coincided with acts like the *Metropolitan Open Spaces Acts* and the *Metropolitan Board of Works Act 1877*, the latter of which allowed for the prohibition of bills and placards and also allowed the making of byelaws to prevent disfigurement in open spaces.[26] Seen from this perspective, outdoor advertising controls form part of the 'avalanche of law' enacted from the middle of the century 'to create new standards of a liveable city' in London that was also gradually spreading beyond the metropolis.[27]

The notion of legislative, regulatory controls was by the 1870s beginning to find support in the press too. However, there was little agreement on whether the issues were over the quality of advertisements, their content or the mere presence of 'puffery' in ever greater amounts. In

[25] *Local Government Act*, 1948 (11 and 12 Geo. 6 c. 26), s. 56.

[26] *The Metropolitan Board of Works Act*, 1877 (40 and 41 Vict. c. 8), s. 15.

[27] Lisa Keller, *Triumph of Order: Democracy and Public Space in New York and London* (Chichester, 2009), p. 102.

1874 *Punch*, having listed examples of vulgar and offensive advertisements, asked if they did not 'constitute a case for the appointment of an Officer in connection with the Board of Works empowered to superintend illustrated advertisements and prohibit all such as are public eye-sores?'[28] In 1877 the *Freeman's Journal*, taking a slightly different line, argued that 'one of the most unmitigated nuisances, street advertising' was to be 'seriously grappled with' again by the *Metropolitan Board of Works*, which had 'resolved to abolish the nuisance'.[29] Though the writer thus 'took for granted' that hoardings and dead walls would soon 'be freed from the glaring and offensive placards and woodcuts which now disfigure them' no bills or byelaws were as yet forthcoming.[30] Indeed, it is debatable whether this sort of total elimination was ever desired, especially by local authorities. By 1892, having gained a suite of new powers over outdoor advertising, the most aggressive action taken by the LCC was to serve notices to a limited number of advertising contractors to take down particular hoardings using the powers contained in the 1882 *Metropolis Management and Buildings Act*, and to limit the size of hoardings to twelve feet, an attitude that suggested the council desired uniformity and order rather than the freeing of all outdoor space from advertising.[31]

There was an emerging sense in newspapers and journals that advertisements should be curtailed and regulated somehow, but as *Punch* and the *Freeman's Journal* illustrate, there was no consensus on quite *why* advertising needed to be controlled beyond general notions of nuisance and disfigurement. Objections were, moreover, balanced by voices, like those in parliament, that saw advertising as a natural part of the commercial environment, but also by those that lauded the spectacle or artistic display. In March 1867, for example, the *Standard* newspaper paid for a seventy-foot-long hoarding on the premises of a brewery on New Oxford Street, which attracted a considerable crowd and saw the billposting company owner, Alexander Scott, lauded in the local press for his skill, which considered him deserving of his '*nom de guerre* ...The Champion Bill Poster'.[32] In 1872, responding to criticism of 'monster advertisements

[28] *Punch*, 'Advertising Offences', 12 September 1874, p. 111.

[29] *Weekly Freeman's Journal*, 3 November 1877, p. 5.

[30] *The British Architect and Northern Engineer*, 27 July 1877, p. 51.

[31] *The Times*, 11 March 1896, p. 13.

[32] *West Middlesex Advertiser and Family Journal*, 23 March 1867, p. 3.

at railway stations' the *Islington Gazette* argued that 'educationally the broadside-wall is a boon; it is the poor man's newspaper, the boy's picture gallery', echoing the idea of 'the poor-man's picture gallery' a phrase in common circulation, usually, though not accurately, attributed to W.T. Stead.[33] They added that anyone who had experience of a railway station could hardly claim the environment could be 'disfigured' by the presence of advertising. The sentiment that some types of location lacked sufficient aesthetic appeal to be prejudiced by advertisements and the question of how such value might be judged would be a recurring feature in debates for the next century.

The idea of poster art as a poor man's picture gallery was not an uncommon argument for outdoor advertising. Yet, the most frequently articulated point of opposition was not outdoor advertising's existence nor a critique of its artistic merits, but the sheer uncontrolled volume of it. Although historians have correctly located the rise of disquiet concerning the invasive and assertive practices of outdoor advertising to a high point of outrage in the press during the 1880s and 1890s, there is a recurring sense from the 1860s onwards that advertising was taking over the entirety of lived space.[34] *Punch* was a consistent critic of outdoor advertising's proliferation, in 1865 wondering when 'the mania for advertising' would stop.[35] In the same year a letter, attributed to the appropriately named 'Anglo-Barnum' glibly suggested the considerable potential of the interior of Westminster Abbey or St Paul's as sites for adverting.[36] In 1868, the magazine placed poster advertising in a more general disquiet about the ubiquitous nature of advertising in all aspects of daily life:

> Where will the mania for advertising carry people? Not merely hoardings, but houses are now covered with advertisements. Puffs are pasted on dead walls and painted upon pavements. Poster bearers everywhere perambulate

[33] *Islington Gazette*, 6 September 1872, p. 3; Stead was repeating a variation phrase in common circulation when he said 'the picture gallery of the English poor is the hoardings of the street' William T. Stead, *The Art of Advertising. Its Theory and Practice Fully Described* (London, 1899), p. 95.

[34] John Hewitt, 'Poster Nasties: Censorship and the Victorian Theatre Poster', in Simon Popple and Vanessa Toulmin (eds), *Visual Delight: Essays on the Popular and Projected Image in the Nineteenth Cent*ury (London, 2000), pp. 154–169 (p. 157).

[35] *Punch*, 'Advertising Atrocities', 14 January 1865, p. 21.

[36] *Punch*, 'The Modern Art of Illumination', 27 May 1865, p. 216.

> the streets and omnibuses are made hideous by the placards which disfigure them. Railways are among the worst offenders in this way their stations are let out to advertising agents and well-nigh every carriage is a vehicle for puffery.[37]

In the same year, with characteristic hyperbole, they returned to the notion of advertising as a kind of secular profanity when one column asked whether the extent of advertising's advance would soon see it assume a genuinely blasphemous medium by producing stained glass windows for churches with 'advertisements in glowing colours'.[38]

Although, we have to be cautious how we interpret newspapers, despite their diverse opinions they nevertheless illustrate the prevalence of similar types of questions to those being asked by *Punch,* expressing concern over the impact of outdoor advertising on the experience of the city. In 1871 a barrister wrote to the editor of the *Morning Post* to complain about a hoarding let by the government to advertisers for 'the privilege of disfiguring it with sensational placards...Surely, sir, it is time that this disgraceful practice of letting out hoardings in our great thoroughfares should be discontinued.[39] In 1872 the *Morning Advertiser* ran a lengthy column bemoaning the ways that 'the architectural effects [of London] were nullified by the efforts of the bill-sticker'. It had 'always been the complaint that St Paul's could not be seen' because of 'the interposition of the inevitable poster-nightmare, the bilious excrescence, hideous as the creation of indigestion'. 'It is of little use' they argued 'that we have been seized by this mania for beautifying London, since at the same time we have fallen prey to this modern element of disfiguration'. Indeed, they expanded upon this idea: 'sensitive persons justly complain of [poster advertising] for its irritating effects on the nervous system'.[40] It had been relatively common for newspapers, as we saw in Chapter 2, to decry posters and hoarding for their obstructive qualities, but both the concerned barrister and the *Morning Advertiser* illustrated a different sentiment: that outdoor advertising was antagonistic to the utility of civic display and planned urban spaces as a kind of public good in a period

[37] *Punch* 'The Art of Advertising', 14 March 1868, p. 119.

[38] *Punch*, 'Ideas on Advertising', 4 April 1868, p. 144.

[39] *Morning Post*, 18 January 1871, p. 3.

[40] *Morning Advertiser*, 13 September 1872, p. 4.

when grand infrastructural development, parks, libraries, art galleries and museums represented a very spatial desire to civilise citizens.[41]

There is, in these objections, a sense that outdoor advertisements were both damaging to the senses as well as disruptive to architecture. As geographer Laura Baker and sociologist Kurt Iveson have both observed, outdoor advertising is loathed by architects and, as I examine in Chapter 5, planners because it is disruptive of the civilising influence of architecture and the social objectives of urban improvement.[42] The idea that advertisements were part of an urban environment that was wearying and bewildering to inhabitants too is itself illustrative of a discourse of urban experience that was leading scientists and the emerging practitioners of sociology to examine the psychological issues associated with the city.[43] As Caroline Arscott has commented, the 1880s was a moment when a general gloom and bleak vision of urban alienation that had developed since the mid-century was offset by the emergence of utopian schemes for urban development. If infrastructural schemes and architectural grandeur represented the moral ambitions of the Victorians, both actually and artistically, their disfigurement held the potential to confound those very aims.[44]

In 1882 the *Illustrated London News* complained that despite London having grown in architectural beauty in the last twenty years, 'many fine positions' were 'disfigured' by placards and advertisements on railway bridges, concluding 'the eye wearies and the heart sickens at the hideous faces and figures that glare at us from these placards…they are a disgrace to the authorities who allow of such displays'. Yet the writer also drew

[41] Douglas A. Reid, 'Playing and Praying', in Martin Daunton (ed), *The Cambridge Urban History of Britain, Vol. 3 1840–1950* (Cambridge, 2000), pp. 745–807 (p. 763). Doyle, *The Changing Functions of Urban Government*, p. 291.

[42] Laura Baker, 'Public Sites Versus Public Sights: The Progressive Response to Outdoor Advertising and the Commercialization of Public Space', *American Quarterly* 59:4 (2007), pp. 1187–213; Kurt Iveson, 'Branded Cities: Outdoor Advertising, Urban Governance, and the Outdoor Media Landscape', *Antipode* 44:1 (2012), pp. 151–174.

[43] Mark Jackson, *The Age of Stress: Science and the Search for Stability* (Oxford, 2013), pp. 34–36; Leif Jerram, *Streetlife: The Untold History of Europe's Twentieth Century* (Oxford, 2011), p. 328; Georg Simmel, *The Metropolis and Mental Life* (1903) for one of the classic studies of urban experience at the turn of the century.

[44] Caroline Arscott, 'The Representation of the City in the Visual Arts', in Martin Daunton (ed), *The Cambridge Urban History of Britain, Vol. 3 1840–1950* (Cambridge, 2000), pp. 811–840 (p. 812).

a line between the interests of commerce and the urban population: 'it seems to be the lot of Englishmen to spend large sums on the improvement of this mighty city, while allowing, at the same time, companies or private persons to step in and deform it'.[45] This association between the interest of private companies working against the experience of urban space, and indeed a certain sense of civic pride was not only evident in London either. In Newtownards, County Down, to the delight of the local newspaper, local magistrate James Brownlow wrote that advertising placards that 'disfigured' the Market House would be removed forthwith because 'it looks bad, but it is especially undesirable at a time of year when a large number of people may be expected to pass through Newtownards'.[46] In 1886 Folkstone banned advertising boards outside its town hall, which had 'long been an eyesore to the public'.[47]

Yet questions of civic beauty were only one part of the more frequent reasons behind criticism of advertisements. At a meeting of the Mersey Dock Board in October 1882, there were revealing disagreements about the renewal of the licence to display 'framed advertisements' on the Liverpool landing stages. Mr Holt, recommending the renewal, added that under the terms of the agreement the committee retained control over the character of the advertisements. Yet there were dissenting voices. Mr Sitt argued that a body like the Dock Board, considering its substantial existing revenues should not allow its 'estate to be disfigured with grotesques and objectionable placards' that were not framed. Mr Gladstone went further, urging the board to allow no advertisements. He commented that 'no one with any sense of what was decorous or proper could walk along the landing stage or the approaches to it without feeling annoyed and vexed at the vulgar obtrusive and offensive advertisements which met him at every turn'. The renewal was carried by ten votes to five, the considerable sum of £600 per year winning out over the more experiential concerns of Sitt and Gladstone.[48]

What the three differing opinions of the members of the Dock Board illustrate is both the emergence of a discourse that questioned the presence of outdoor adverting, even in a relatively commercial environment,

[45] *Illustrated London News*, 19 August 1882, p. 18.

[46] *Newtownards Chronicle & Co. Down Observer*, 9 September 1882, p. 3.

[47] *Folkestone Express, Sandgate, Shorncliffe & Hythe Advertiser*, 20 March 1886, p. 5.

[48] *Liverpool Mercury*, 14 October 1882, p. 8.

but also the lack of agreement about what the actual issue at stake was. There remained a certain section of society who saw outdoor advertising simply as part of the commercial space of the city, either as a vital component or with a degree of ambivalence. Others saw an issue in the proliferation of untidy, unartistic or even indecent posters and wished to encourage some combination of higher standards, stricter regulation or greater censorship. Another strand of thinking argued that advertising was inherently objectionable and wished for it to be reduced in great measure, although few argued for its total elimination. Advertisers themselves tended to make their case by appealing to the idea that poster art was a chance to brighten drab cities and even educate the average urban dweller. Indeed, they would cleave closely to this argument for years to come. In 1881 the *Sporting Gazette* contended that posters and handbills featuring *The Magazine of Art* cover by artist Hubert Herkomer would 'raise the taste of the people' and unlike the 'daubs we now see on our walls, refine and not disgust'.[49] As John Hewitt has argued, poster art in the later years of the nineteenth century still utilised 'fine art and fine artists' until the turn of the century when this tendency gave way to what was recognisably commercial art.[50] Yet, there was little evidence that the high standards were being maintained in anything but exceptional cases. In 1896 an article entitled 'Bill-Posting as Fine Art' in *The Saturday Review* argued that poster advertising in London was 'ugly in design and coarse in execution, feeble in line and harsh in colour; and they might easily be simple strong and artistically rich without losing any of their attractiveness as advertisements'.[51] The periodical, *The Poster*, published between 1898 and 1900, held that the majority of bills displayed around cities were such eyesores that they did not truly deserve their designation as posters.[52]

The sheer volume of posters produced though meant that an ordered and tasteful display of advertising was, for the moment, a mere pipedream. Indeed, to argue that the issue facing poster advertising was simply

[49] 'The Man About Town' *The Sporting Gazette*, vol. XIX, no. 990, 30 April 1881, p. 461.

[50] John Hewitt, 'Designing the Poster in England, 1890–1914', *Early Popular Visual Culture* 5:1 (2007), pp. 57–70 (p. 57).

[51] *The Saturday Review of Politics, Literature, Science, and Art*, 31 July 1886, p. 152.

[52] John Hewitt, '"The Poster" and the Poster in England in the 1890s', *Victorian Periodicals Review* 35:1 (2002), pp. 37–62.

one of quality was to miss both the point of many objections and to swim against the trends within the industry. Between 1882 and 1888 *Punch* parodied aspects of advertising culture under the infrequent title 'How We Advertise Now' or, in the last instant 'Nowadays', that focused upon the incessant and intrusive nature of advertising culture, particularly the increasingly sensational and lurid content of posters. One much cited example from 1887, whilst also depicting the still-present physical nuisance of sandwich men and gawking crowds, shows a wall covered in posters depicting murder, ghouls and, perhaps just as offensively to the Victorian eye, women's scantily clad legs.[53] In 1888 in a poem that accompanied an image of a devil as a bill sticker pasting-up advertisements for crime theatre and penny dreadfuls, *Punch* imagined the demon musing that it was strange that a city that imagined itself as civilised allowed such 'liberal licence' on posters, concluding: 'these mural monstrosities, reeking of crime, flaring horridly forth amidst squalor and grime. Must have an effect which will tell in good time, upon legions of dull-witted toilers'.[54] However, as ever with *Punch*, the cartoon takes aim at both advertisers and the critics who believed they held the potential to stir up incivility in the labouring classes.

The content of advertisements was, even though *Punch* might lampoon the sentiment, becoming an issue because of the way the governing classes imagined it negatively influenced the lower classes. Posters of the period often featured 'a crude sensationalism, and in some cases the acts of violence depicted sought to convey an indirectly sexual thrill' that was parodied so effectively in *Punch*.[55] Indeed, advertising in general was increasingly criticised for its content and became

[53] *Punch*, 'Our Recreations, or How We Advertise Now', 28 January 1882, p. 37 parodies the style of newspaper classifieds; 'How We Advertise Now', 5 November 1887, p. 216 is a comment on a popular dental product advertisement; 'How We Advertise Nowadays', 14 July 1888, p. 21 is a pastiche of Millais' famous 'Bubbles' advertisement that notes the tendency for quack remedies in advertising. 'How We Advertise Now', 3 December 1887, p. 262 is a full-page street scene (described above) displaying a carriage assailed by crowds and sandwich men in front of a giant wall of grotesque advertisements that have become somewhat emblematic of the period. Cited in Taylor, 'Written in the Skies', p. 793 and Hewitt, 'Poster Nasties', p. 157.

[54] *Punch*, 'Horrible London: Or, the Pandemonium of Posters', 13 October 1888, vol. 95, p. 170.

[55] Sheldon, *History of Poster Advertising*, p. 65.

the target of the *Indecent Advertisements Bill* in 1889.[56] The prelude to this bill was a period of hypersensitivity over purportedly lewd posters in the 1880s. In 1885, national and provincial newspapers reported that there had been protests from Bishop Alford, backed-up by subsequent letters from concerned citizens, about posters for the Royal Aquarium and Winter Gardens featuring a 'highly-coloured colossal picture of an almost-naked woman lying in a lascivious attitude'.[57] The Bishop's horror was one of several incidents involving advertising posters in the period that whipped-up a variety of sentiments in the press. However, the *Indecent Advertisements Act*, which became law in 1890 was aimed less at the types of titillating indecency that animated the Bishop and his supporters than it was at reducing advertisements, particularly hand bills, that dealt with sexually transmitted diseases. The Earl of Meath, proposing the bill, reported these forms of advertising were 'inducements to promiscuous sexual intercourse… [that are] contaminating the minds of the young'.[58] In this sense the Act falls into that category of later Victorian legislation and state intervention that Jeffery Weeks and Judith Walkowitz have shown laid claim to the regulation of individuals' morality.[59] Obscenity, as Lynda Nead concluded in her case study of attempts to suppress obscene publications in the 1860s, was 'modernity's other', the counterpoint to the impulse to improve, regulate and order Victorian London.[60] What was important about the Act was not its objectives—indeed this sort of crusading morality, especially over popular and print culture was quite common amongst a certain section of the Victorian political class[61]—rather, it is that it targeted the actual content of adverts. In debating the Bill it was acknowledged that 'neither the *Metropolitan Police Act* of

[56] Hansard, HL, 8 April 1889, vol. 334, cc. 1761–1766.

[57] *Waterford Mirror and Tramore Visitor*, 12 November 1885, p. 4; *The Times*, 9 October 1885, p. 5; *The Times*, 28 October 1885, p. 13.

[58] Hansard, HL, 8 April 1889, vol. 334, cc. 1762.

[59] Jeffrey Weeks, *Sex, Politics, and Society: The Regulation of Sexuality Since* 1800 (London, 1989).

Judith Walkowitz, *City of Dreadful Delight: Narratives of Sexual Danger in Late-Victorian London* (Chicago, 1992).

[60] Nead, *Victorian Babylon*, p. 149.

[61] For example, with respect to visual culture see: Brenda Assael, 'Art or Indecency? Tableaux Vivants on the London Stage and the Failure of Late Victorian Moral Reform', *Journal of British Studies* 45:4 (2006), pp. 744–758.

1839 nor the Act of 1847 touches this question [of preventing indecent advertisements] ... the only thing that can be done is to charge a person who is circulating it with causing annoyance'.[62] The older acts which had targeted advertisements for their physical nuisance no longer reflected the concerns the guardians of public morals had over the functioning of commercial culture in urban space.

The legislation dealing with indecency, though important, is perhaps more interesting here for what it tells us about how the less tangible effects of advertisements in public spaces were being imagined. In 1890 more Royal Aquarium posters, this time advertising trapeze artist Adelaide 'Zaeo' Wieland were the subject of outrage from the crusading National Vigilance Association (NVA) because, by careful use of colour, they appeared to show the performer's bare arms and legs in a provocative pose. Their NVA's actual goal was the revocation of the Aquarium's licence by the newly formed LCC, based on their belief that it was a den of prostitution and immorality, and the new Act was seized upon as a vehicle to make their case.[63] Although the case was dismissed, as theatre historian Tracy Davis has argued, the particular pose and composition of the Zaeo poster encoded notions of feminine physicality that, unlocked by the male gaze, brought sex into public places.[64] It encapsulated the fear that the unregulated competition for the brief attention of the citizen's eye in crowded urban spaces, inevitably produced increasingly lurid and sexualised displays. The furore, though, has perhaps outpaced the actual significance of the Zaeo scandal, which was as much mocked as it was taken as a serious threat by the press and commentators of the time. *Punch*, responding to the 1885 complaints from Bishop Alford, had mocked the prudery of the objection with its typical faux correspondence, in which a crusading 'Model of Mankind' had gone in search of the offending poster only to be left disappointed.[65] The *Telegraph* too characterised critics 'discovering enormity in the cartoons' as Justice OVERDO and Rabbi ZEAL-O'-THE-LAND BUSY [original

[62] Hansard, HL, 8 April 1889, vol. 334, cc. 1761–1762.

[63] Richard Anthony Baker, *British Music Hall: An Illustrated Hist*ory (Barnsley, 2014), p. 44; Tracy C. Davis, 'Sex in Public Places: The Zaeo Aquarium Scandal and the Victorian Moral Majority', *Theatre History Studies* 10 (1990), pp. 1–13.

[64] Davis, *Sex in Public Places*, p. 12.

[65] *Punch*, 'Babes on the Wood', 14 November 1885, p. 230.

capitals].[66] Even Richardson Evans, outdoor advertising's nemesis-in-waiting, branded the outcry 'foolish enough'.[67] Indeed, in the same period the greater calls for censorship, especially during the frenzy over The Ripper murders, were aimed not at sexual indecency but at the corrupting influence of posters depicting violence and murder.[68]

The central issue that these scandals reveal is the ways the poster was being considered as something with which the public interacted, in certain cases in a very material way. The Zaeo posters themselves were, where in physical reach of the public, 'decorated in a most immoral and indecent manner' drawing fines for the ribald graffiti artists.[69] The outcry against them was symptomatic both of the vocal nature of late-Victorian prudes, but also an evolving view of how the population experienced and were influenced by their surroundings. Posters, like cheap literature or sensational theatre, contained images that 'cultivated a new, excited sensibility' especially to allegedly suggestible, lower-class audiences.[70] If this was, as proponents of liberal governmentality have suggested a period when the control of urban space sought to produce a civil and ordered society, the types of sensational outdoor advertising discussed here were being presented as a disordering, even corrupting presence.[71] In 1843, when Thomas Carlyle had objected to 'this all-deafening blast of Puffery, of poor Falsehood grown necessitous', his argument had been that advertising as a practice represented immodest boasting, degrading the character of both manufacturer and society.[72] That the British tolerated posters and advertising vans as a fact of the urban environment was a symptom of their moral decline, not the cause of it. Yet by the end of the century those who feared for the nation's morals, like the NVA and the

[66] *Daily Telegraph and Courier*, 10 October 1890, p. 5.

[67] Richardson Evans, *The Age of Disfigurement* (London, 1893), p. 1.

[68] *West London Observer*, 7 November 1891, p. 7.

[69] Greater London Record Office (now London Metropolitan Archives), 'Testimony of W.A Coote', London County Council Minutes (LCC/MIN) 10,891, 2 October 1890, quoted in Davis, *Sex in Public Places*, p. 2.

[70] Nead, *Victorian Babylon*, p. 150.

[71] Chris Otter, 'Making Liberalism Durable: Vision and Civility in the Late-Victorian City', *Social History* 27:1 (2002), pp. 1–15.

[72] Thomas Carlyle, *Past and Present* (London, 1843), p. 303.

Earl of Meath were plotting a more engaged relationship between advertising, lived space and the public that revolved around an understanding of posters' effects that went beyond their mere physical presence.

The immediate importance of the outcry over indecency, though, was that it came at the same time that attitudes against 'disfigurement' that surfaced in the 1870s had grown into a noticeable groundswell in popular print.[73] Local corporations were slowly showing an interest in regulating hoardings and advertising stations, there was a growing opinion that poster advertising was disfiguring the built environment, a formerly uninterested parliament had approved a set of statutory controls on outdoor advertising and its content, whilst moral crusaders had whipped-up a storm over the Zaeo case and were threatening to promote a censorship bill.[74] In November 1890 showing similar pragmatism that they had in the 1850s and 1860s *The Billposter*, one of two industry journals claimed 'we are living in precarious times…constant attempts have been made to interfere with our trade and if we are to be so persistently harassed, profits must diminish. Unless we can secure popular support, we shall certainly lose in the coming conflict'.[75] In the same year there were a number of public calls for the institution of a board of censors to govern advertising content. *The Globe*, in May 1890, argued that many poster advertisements were 'particularly offensive, not only to the aesthetic sense but to the sense of decency….a standard of propriety must at least be raised and by the aid of judicious censor or board of inspection must be sustained'.[76]

Seeking to maintain as much discretionary control as possible, towards the end of 1890 the London Billposters' Protection Association, later joined by the UKBPA created a censorship committee of their own to monitor the content of posters they were asked to print.[77] The make-up of the committee would change over the years, adding in representation from theatres and the provinces over time, the former typically being the source of the greatest complaints about lurid images, but they proved

[73] James Taylor, 'Written in the Skies: Advertising, Technology and Modernity in Britain Since 1885', *Journal of British Studies* 55 (2016), pp. 750–780 (pp. 763–765).

[74] *West London Observer*, 7 November 1891, p. 7.

[75] *The Billposter*, November 1890 quoted in Sheldon, *A History of Poster Advertising*, p. 58.

[76] *The Globe*, 3 May 1890, p. 1.

[77] *Daily Telegraph and Courier*, 10 October 1890, p. 5.

surprisingly strict.[78] Despite the reservations of a number of newspapers about the capabilities of the committee to govern their own industry, they appear to have enjoyed a fair degree of success amongst a fraternity of billposting companies who recognised that they enjoyed little support amongst the powerful.[79] This balance between governmental pressure and billposters' pragmatism would become a recurring feature of the relationship until after the Second World War. Advertising companies fought to retain their rights to practice their profession as freely as possible but reacted swiftly when they felt an argument had tipped against them. Although calls for censorship never entirely died down, by taking a strict line and over time expanding the remit of the committee to the provinces and to the assessment of theatre posters, the billposting associations were able to deflect the calls for independent adjudication or any extension of statutory censorship.[80]

The creation of the censorship committee demonstrates, as it had in the consolidation of the industry, the creation of the directories and the move towards advertising stations, the pragmatism and commercial savvy of the billposters' associations. Maintaining their position was a balancing act between the rapacious hunger of commercial culture for advertising space and ever-greater spectacle, and evolving understandings of what public space was for. The issue of indecency was itself not a particularly significant problem, despite the furore over some fairly minor incidents being well remembered. The reaction of the billposters, however, reveals just how precarious their position appeared to have become by the 1880s and how powerfully a general sentiment against uncontrolled advertising was being expressed.

A Golden Age? Local Control and Sky Signs

A number of authors have referred to the 1890s as perhaps the golden age of advertising, when advertising enterprise was at its most inventive, whilst advertisers were bound by few codes either moral or statutory.[81] The

[78] Sheldon, *A History of Poster Advertising*, pp. 62–65.

[79] For sceptical takes from newspapers the *Aberdeen Evening Express*, 11 October 1890, p. 2 is typical in its witheringly sarcastic assessment of the potential effectiveness of self-censorship.

[80] Sheldon, *A History of Poster Advertising*, pp. 62–65.

[81] Turner, *The Shocking History of Advertising*, p. 132.

passing of both the acts regulating rating and indecent advertisements nevertheless signalled the beginning of a period of increased activism from local authorities with regard to establishing regulatory powers over advertising. Advertisements on railways were a much commented upon aspect of posters' spread and in 1891 *The Central London Railway Act* meant that the railway's proprietors must seek permission from the relevant local authority to display adverts within sight of the street in both the County and City of London.[82] In 1892 the *Newcastle-upon-Tyne Improvement Act* classified buildings in such a way that advertisers would need permission to erect a hoarding or new advertising station. A year later York Corporation failed to get a bill that would give them the power to refuse permission for or define the size and construction of any structure used for advertising past consultation with citizens, whilst Leeds were more successful with a clause in their improvement act which restricted the height of hoardings.[83] Section 30 of the *Thames Conservancy Bill* in 1893 saw the body that managed the river request the powers to restrict all advertising on the water and banks of the Thames, a power that was stricken from the final version.[84]

Despite the mixed success of attempts to extend powers, over the remaining years of the century a number of local corporations across England were active in expanding the regulations already afforded to them. Cardiff Corporation (1894) and Matlock Urban District Council (1898) included wide-ranging subsections in general bills that dealt with advertising vans, permission to erect hoardings and prohibiting sky signs (signs that projected above the roofs of buildings). Others like Bridlington (1894), South Shields and Southend-on-Sea (both 1895) introduced acts that simply allowed them to make byelaws that might govern the erection of hoardings for advertising.[85] These acts did not all pass without modification, facing opposition both from MPs and from the lobbying of the billposters and advertising bodies. Having struggled to exert any influence over the passage of the 1889 acts, the billposters' associations were more active in opposing later bills and the changes to bills demonstrate

[82] *Central London Railways Act*, 1891 (54 and 54 Vict. c. 196), s. 54 and s. 68.

[83] Sheldon, *The History of Poster Advertising*, pp. 135–137.

[84] *The Times*, 18 November 1893, p. 3.

[85] Sheldon, *The History of Poster Advertising*, pp. 135–138.

both their activism and the gap between the views of the national legislature and local governments. When Brighouse Corporation proposed a bill to restrict sky signs, ban advertising vans and prevent the use or erection of structures used for advertising without the corporation's permission, amendments made in parliament limited the bill to newly constructed sites and struck-out a section that allowed hoardings to be removed if deemed unsafe.[86]

Perhaps the most revealing development before the very end of the century though was the reaction to sky signs throughout 1890 and 1891, studied in detail as part of a wider examination of advertising in the skies by historian James Taylor.[87] Sky signs were wood or metal frames featuring the names and slogans of products that were positioned on top of buildings in such a way that the letters stood out against the sky. 'The result' according to advertising historian Ernest Turner 'was that the roofs of London presented a crazed alphabetic silhouette calculated to make any painter throw away his brushes'.[88] Sky signs, unlike other forms of advertising though, garnered considerable attention, and thus swift and decisive censure. Though they began to appear in London around 1886, sky signs seem to have attracted little comment before 1890. Yet in a matter of weeks their allegedly damaging effect on the experience of citizens and the urban environment became a topic of considerable discussion both in the capital and outside.[89] London's *The Graphic* newspaper commented that:

> Even the boldest [advertiser] hesitated until quite recently to use the firmament as a background for their vulgarities...the sky sign is the most hateful infliction of all, depriving as it does the disgusted wayfarer of the very last rest for his weary eyes.[90]

[86] Select Committee on Police and Sanitary Regulations Bills: Special Report, Proceedings, 5 July 1895, vol. 12, XII.113; *Brighouse News*, 11 May 1895, p. 2.

[87] Taylor, 'Written in the Skies'.

[88] Ernest Turner, *The Shocking History of Advertising* (Harmondsworth, 1965), p. 110.

[89] Taylor, 'Written in the Skies', p. 757. In September 1890 the Western Mail claimed that they had been invented and patented in either 1886 or 1887. *Western Mail*, 4 September 1890, p. 4.

[90] *The Graphic*, 6 September 1890, p. 4.

In Birmingham, too, in July 1890 a disgruntled citizen similarly invoked the idea that in colonising the sky, advertisers had crossed a line:

> The lot of people who are compelled to live in the city is generally bad enough as regards their surroundings without having the one beautiful part of their prospect – that of the sky – defaced...If our regulations are so deficient as to leave our City Council without power in this matter it is time for an additional rule to be enacted and enforced ...If 'signs in the heavens' such as these are to be multiplied they can only be signs of the vulgarity of those who dwell below them and a warning to associations for the promotion of art that our newly aroused enthusiasm for beauty and sweetness is unreal.[91]

The letter also illustrates the way citizens were internalising questions of the value of urban experience and the local state's role in regulating and preserving aspects of cities that were beneficial to citizens. In asking whether a legislative solution might be necessary, the correspondent lent on notions that the role of empowered local authorities was the production of urban environments that, if not necessarily objectively beautiful, should certainly not be allowed to get worse. As Taylor observes, the way opposition to sky signs was being framed shows the emergence of two developing aspects of these ideas about how urban life should be governed. On the one hand, the expansion of structures above roof-level threatened the levels of light and air that citizens might enjoy, which were aspects of urban experience that the LCC and other local authorities were beginning to tackle with legislation regulating building heights, clean air laws and, later, measurements of sunlight.[92] The reaction to sky signs thus shows, as did the fledgling attempts at advertising control, the creeping ambition of the local state to regulate space in ever-more detailed ways that linked more abstract notions of experience to the existing and more tangible discourses of public health. On the other hand, the more

[91] *Birmingham Daily Post*, 15 July 1890, p. 4.

[92] Taylor, 'Written in the Skies', p. 768; on attempts to control pollution and air quality see: Peter Brimblecombe, *The Big Smoke: A History of Air Pollution in London Since Medieval Times* (London, 1988); Catherine Bowler and Peter Brimblecombe, 'Control of Air Pollution in Manchester Prior to the Public Health Act, 1875', *Environment and History* 6:1 (2000), pp. 71–98; Stephen Mosley, *The Chimney of the World: A History of Smoke Pollution in Victorian and Edwardian Manchester* (London, 2009). On buildings impinging upon light and air, Chris Otter, 'Making Liberalism Durable: Vision and Civility in the Late-Victorian City', *Social History* 27:1 (2002), pp. 1–15 (p. 8).

abstract notion that the sky should be preserved depicted the sky as urban dwellers' sole connection to nature in an increasingly exhausting and bewildering modern city.[93]

This examination of the speed with which the ban on sky sings was adopted—the legislation became law in late 1891—against the slow progress of other legislation dealing with outdoor advertising and opposition from parliament, also reveals a lingering ambivalence about the function and value of extant urban spaces, which bedevilled proponents of advertising control until the 1950s. The Birmingham correspondent suggested that without the beauty of the sky, life was 'generally bad enough' in the city. The condemnation and consensus over sky signs thus exposed a lack of agreement on what level of commercialism was appropriate in towns and cities, and, indeed, what value mundane spaces really had. A poem in satirical magazine and some-time *Punch* rival *Fun* entitled 'Those Horrid Sky Signs' quoted *The Globe* in remarking 'there are signs visible on the horizon of public opinion…[that] "sky signs" will not be tolerated in this unfortunate metropolis' before going on to lampoon the sudden vehemence of anti-sky sign sentiment.[94] *The Ipswich Journal* characterised the debate as aesthetes against 'the commercial', whilst in Cardiff's *Western Mail*, the correspondent reporting back on happenings in London offered the opinion that sky signs were 'the indignant protest of anguished athletes', adding that:

> These glaring tokens of enterprise may offend the artistic sensibilities of some people, but I do not think a case can be made out for interference. London is getting so unwieldy that the only chance of attracting attention that is left to a tradesman is to go higher.[95]

Despite these dissenting voices, the uproar about sky signs was picked-up by the LCC and the construction of any more of the structures without permission was banned under the *London Sky Signs Act* 1891, a prohibition affirmed and redefined in 1893 and again in 1894. This impetus was taken-up piecemeal in individual bills by local corporations and extended

93 Taylor, 'Written in the Skies', pp. 768–769.

94 Alvin Sullivan, *British Literary Magazines: The Victorian and Edwardian Age, 1837–1913* (London, 1984), p. 135.

95 *The Ipswich Journal*, 6 September 1890, p. 8; *Western Mail*, 4 September 1890, p. 4.

in permissive fashion to all local authorities by the *Public Health Act* 1907, and 154 had taken advantage of the new law in England and Wales by 1910.[96]

The pace with which the sky signs issue was brought to a conclusion is illustrative of both the strength of broad aesthetic arguments against outdoor advertising and the growing remit of the local state's—particularly the LCC's—attempts to exert regulatory control over urban space. The swiftness with which the LCC picked-up the issue, recognised the opportunity and rode the wave of vocal sentiment to effectively gain control of the spread of sky signs, shows a growing concern about outdoor advertising's role in cities, but also shows just how exceptional the response to sky signs was. By showing how swiftly action could be taken when consensus over the value of an uncluttered sky was recognised, the case conversely reveals how difficult the question of how urban space should be governed and what it was for really was. Moreover, the actual use of the new powers by the LCC further demonstrates that the desire for the powers was, at this stage, very much about the potential to remove signs, not the desire to supress them. After two years of the 1891 Act's operation 812 signs had been reported to the LCC, but only 247 of these were removed, with a further 169 licenced, but scheduled for removal by 1897. Of the remaining number, 340 were judged to fall beyond the remit of the legislation, whilst 56 'evaded the act' by changing the materials used. Although the redefinition of 'sky sign' by parliament in 1893 brought, by the estimation of SCAPA, close to 3,000 signs into consideration for removal, a short time after, only forty-three had been removed, 157 had been licenced until 1899, whilst the council continued to show, in the opinion of critics, considerable 'latitude of interpretation'.[97]

[96] Taylor, 'Written in the Skies', p. 757; original act *The London Sky Signs Act*, 1891 (54 and 55 Vict. c. 78) amended by *The London County Council (General Powers) Act*, 1893 (56 and 57 Vict. c. 221), s. 17 and *The London Building Act*, 1894 (57 and 58 Vict. c. 213), s. 125.

[97] *A Beautiful World: The Journal of the Society for Checking the Abuses of Public Advertising*, 3, p. 89.

Conclusion

Although there was still little agreement about the place of advertisements as an aspect of the built environment by the time of the sky signs outcry, the period beginning in the 1870s ushered in a phase where several strands of opposition to outdoor advertising had begun to emerge and, by the 1890s it had coalesced in character around several opinions. In October 1890 Richardson Evans, the driving force behind the formation of SCAPA three years later, was spurred by the sky signs outcry to publish his essay 'The Age of Disfigurement' in the *National Review*, to generally favourable comment in the press.[98] Evans argued that advertisements, though they had their place as part of the economy, were disfiguring the environment and prejudicial to the experience of both town and country. He contended that the only way to control them was extend full regulatory powers to local government to prohibit outdoor advertisements, the scheduling of scenes of remarkable beauty or interest, and a tax on advertising posters.[99] Evans' and SCAPA's arguments are covered in greater detail in the following chapter, but his central points encapsulated the dominant issues of outdoor advertising control and captured the tone of the debate that had emerged from the second half of the nineteenth century.

Outdoor advertisements were no longer seen as merely a physical nuisance and the nature of the industry—to seek more spectacular settings and displays—clashed with the broad patterns of civic improvement that encompassed both planned architectural display and the regulation of extant spaces. This was especially visible in London, where the newly formed LCC was beginning to take action, but it was also emerging in provincial settings, if at an understandably slower pace. No local authority as yet showed any desire for prohibition; indeed, many seem to have welcomed the additional income from advertisements on their own property and the chance to rate advertising stations more effectively after 1889. What the early attempts to pass bills that allowed corporations and councils to control advertising does show though is the increasingly

[98] Richardson Evans, 'The Age of Disfigurement' first published in the *National Review*, October 1890, he stated that he was spurred into action by the sky signs issue in the republished version of the essay: Richardson Evans, *The Age of Disfigurement* (London, 1893), p. 27.

[99] Evans, *The Age of Disfigurement*, pp. 20–21.

detailed and comprehensive tendencies of local authorities to regulate their towns and cities. Outdoor advertising control, though seemingly insignificant in the broader histories of cities, sat at the nexus of regimes of regulation, policing and liberal governance. Though it was very much still embedded within very physical notions of obstruction and public nuisance and would remain so, outdoor advertising was being challenged by patterns of governance situated in questions about what urban space was for, for its effect upon the morals and well-being of the population, as well as for its broader influence on society. Though any new regulatory powers were used in an apparently judicious manner, a growing set of voices asked whether advertisements and their content were prejudicial to the experience of certain spaces. As the following chapter argues, the opponents of outdoor advertising argued that they disrupted civic display or disfigured by their very presence, not merely for their content. These voices, at least by the turn of the century, were still tempered by the piecemeal nature of urban change in Victorian cities. Yet they bought into an emerging set of questions about the role of urban space and the expectations upon and duties of the state to shape and regulate it for the good of the population.

CHAPTER 4

SCAPA, Amenity and the Value of the Environment

Abstract This chapter discusses the consolidation of legislation that protected rural environments, and architecturally and historically valuable buildings, as well as examining the emergence of the term 'amenity' as a key idea in spatial governance in the twentieth century between 1890 and the 1930s. It focuses much of its attention on opposition group SCAPA, using an examination of society's character and campaigns, alongside their rise and subsequent decline, to understand the trajectory of specific legislative controls on outdoor advertising, as well as the issues that emerged within this fledgling system. It shows how symbolic victories at Edinburgh and Dover and a general buzz of regulatory activism from local authorities pushed towards the implementation of the 1907 *ARA and subsequent acts, but also shows how these acts were vague and showed little regard for ordinary urban spaces.*

Keywords SCAPA · Preservationists · Amenity · Rural · Heritage · Planning

J. Greenhalgh, *Injurious Vistas: The Control of Outdoor Advertising, Governance and the Shaping of Urban Experience in Britain, 1817–1962*, Palgrave Studies in Economic History,
https://doi.org/10.1007/978-3-030-79018-9_4

In 1890, spurred into action by the growth of advertising and enlivened by the sky signs outcry, Richardson Evans declared in *The Age of Disfigurement* that 'no one would take me seriously if I did not insist on the necessity of forming an association'.[1] Accordingly, in 1893 at the urging of architect Alfred Waterhouse the National Society for Checking Abuses of Public Advertising (SCAPA) was formed with the aim of opposing 'disfigurement in town and country…to purge the streets and country ways, the fields and riverbanks' of advertisements'.[2] SCAPA, though never an organisation that garnered mass support or a large membership, were instrumental in the expansion of control over and changes to the practices of outdoor advertising before the Second World War.[3] Their successes were most notable in the first twenty-five years of the new century, during which they focused their attention on the elimination of posters and billboards 'which would disfigure the natural beauty of the landscape'.[4] SCAPA's activism was central to the passage of the pivotal 1907 *Advertisements Regulation Act (ARA)* and its successors, as well as a number of other important pieces of legislation. They exerted considerable influence in reducing the presence of roadside billboards and, by the time their influence and energy began to wane during the 1930s, they had made significant progress in curtailing advertisements in the countryside and in historic settings.[5]

Although an avowedly aesthetic and preservationist organisation in many respects, as Paul Readman has shown, SCAPA and the proponents of advertising control were much more than merely conservative and

[1] Richardson Evans, *The Age of Disfigurement* (London, 1893) originally 1890 in the *New Review*.

[2] 'The Advertising Plague', *The Times*, Richardson Evans, 18 November 1892, p. 12 and repeated multiple times in general purposes of the society in London Metropolitan Archives (LMA)/A/SCA 01 and 02, Society for Checking Abuses of Public Advertising, 1892–1952 archive. SCAPA would later expand their campaigns to littering.

[3] In June 1894 SCAPA's *Beautiful World* journal claimed membership was at 730: *A Beautiful World: The Journal of the Society for Checking the Abuses of Public Advertising* 3 (1894), p. 121.

[4] Richardson Evans, *An Account of the SCAPA Society* (London, 1927), pp. 80–84 and 364; Cyril Sheldon, *History of Poster Advertising* (London, 1937), pp. 168–171.

[5] Clarence Moran, *The Business of Advertising* (Abingdon, 1905), p. 121; Terry Nevett, *Advertising in Britain*: A History (London, 1982), p. 161; Malcolm V. Speakman, *Shell's England: Corporate patronage and English Art in Shell Posters of the 1930*s (PhD Thesis, University of Manchester 2014), ch. 2, passim.

anti-modern in their outlook.[6] The tendency has been to see SCAPA's project as tied up with a certain sense of nationalism and rural nostalgia, but this chapter illustrates the complexity and sometimes contradictions of SCAPA's motives and campaigns. Without dismissing these points entirely, this chapter argues that the central emerging notion around which SCAPA framed their protection of 'aspect' and 'sight' was the utility of certain environments to the nation and its public, which—alongside emergent languages of planning and lived experience—gradually placed the notion of amenity at the centre of debates.[7] Nor do I argue that SCAPA were solely preservationists, although they had much in common with the ideas of preservationist organisations. The thrust of SCAPA's campaign was about finding an accommodation between the experience of valuable environments and modern advertising practices that limited the spaces into which commercial culture might expand, not eliminating advertisements as a matter of principle.

SCAPA's extensive records and publications here provide an account of their progress, successes and changing attitudes that form a window into the interior of outdoor advertising's most vociferous and successful opponent from 1893 until the Second World War. The examination of the society's character in this chapter, alongside an account of their rise and subsequent decline, mirrors the trajectory of specific legislative controls on outdoor advertising, as well as the issues that emerged within this fledgling system. In the first section the chapter examines SCAPA's motivations and tactics leading to the passing in 1907 of the first act aimed at placing outdoor advertising in its proper place within urban and rural landscapes. In this first section symbolic victories at Edinburgh and Dover and a general buzz of regulatory activism from local authorities pushed towards the implementation of the 1907 *ARA*, but also witnessed the first uses of the term amenity. The second section deals with the centrality of the concept of amenity and its lineage as a term of legal importance for planning. This section places the 1907 *ARA* in a

[6] Paul Readman, 'Preserving the English Landscape, c.1870–1914', *Cultural and Social History* 5:2 (2008), pp. 197–218.

[7] John Hewitt, 'The "Nature" and "Art" of Shell Advertising in the Early 1930s', *Journal of Design History* 5:2 (1992), pp. 121–139; David Matless, *Landscape and Englishness* (London, 1998), pp. 25–35, 47–52; Paul Readman 'Landscape Preservation, "Advertising Disfigurement", and English National Identity c.1890–1914', *Rural History* 12:1 (2001), pp. 61–83.

wider context of contemporary legislation and reveals advertising control as just one aspect of changing governmental views on how rural and urban environments were valued, managed and used as a national and public good. Anticipating the fifth chapter, I argue that amenity's meaning was changing to reflect a philosophy that conceived of, although in a rather general manner, certain public rights to enjoy useful and picturesque spaces. Amenity and its discussion thus paralleled far-reaching discussions of public recreation and national well-being. The third section examines the implementation of the 1907 Act and the variety of ways that SCAPA opposed outdoor advertising in various settings to show both the success of their non-legislative tactics and the way the general discourse of advertising control became rooted in the protection of subjectively valuable, historic and rural settings at the expense of more mundane, specifically urban environments.

Symbolic Victories and Local Regulation

In their objections to outdoor advertising and proposed solutions SCAPA were the embodiment of the concerns about posters and advertising stations that had begun to appear in the twenty years preceding their formation. Their aims were: regulatory powers for local authorities, preferably absolute or subject to appeal; the scheduling of 'scenes of remarkable beauty or interest' against 'desecration'; a tax on advertising posters; and the creation of awareness of the issue by informing and encouraging a proactive public consciousness.[8] They are most often characterised as one of the body of preservationist societies founded by a certain aesthetic elite that formed throughout the later part of the nineteenth century. This description is hardly unfair; with a membership that never seems to have risen much above 700 many of whom fell squarely into the artistic and aesthetic community they were never a movement that saw the benefits of mass appeal.[9] Though they proved influential in fermenting public disquiet and pushing for legislative changes,

[8] Evans, *The Age of Disfigurement*, pp. 20–21.

[9] In June 1894 SCAPA's *Beautiful World* journal claimed membership was at 730: *A Beautiful World: The Journal of the Society for Checking the Abuses of Public Advertising*, 3 (1894), p. 121. There are no other discernible figures but given the limited appeal and recruitment ambitions of the organisation it seems unlikely they would have risen much above that figure.

SCAPA never intended nor wanted to be a mass membership organisation. Indeed, some members believed that ordinary people's indifference to advertising was 'only another word on our side, for it shows the degradation they [advertisements] have wrought'.[10] Powerful allies included Prime Minister Lord Rosebery, who, speaking to the Academy Dinner in June 1894 confirmed his opposition to outdoor advertising recalling a train journey from Manchester where 'the whole of a pleasing landscape had been ruined by appeals to the public'.[11] Against this backdrop, by 1901 SCAPA numbered the Lord Mayor of London, the Archbishop of Canterbury, at least 24 MPs, the Vice Chancellors of both Oxford and Cambridge, as well as the directors of the British and Natural History museums amongst a body of prominent and influential supporters.[12]

The label preservationist, though appropriate, can nevertheless be a touch misleading. Landscape preservation societies had begun to emerge over the course of the nineteenth century with bodies like the Commons Protection Society (CPS) in 1865 and the National Trust in 1895, alongside SCAPA themselves. Preservationist organisations before 1914 bear something of a stigma rooted in a nationalist and rural nostalgia, and historians have argued that they possessed little appeal and influence, or lacked an appreciation of the realities of modern spatial governance.[13] This latter contention places them in contrast to later movements like the Council for the Preservation of Rural England (CPRE), which stood 'not [for] a conservative protection of the old against the new, but an attempt to plan a landscape simultaneously modern and traditional under the guidance of an expert public authority'.[14] This difference is, however, a little more subtle than it might seem. As Readman has argued, SCAPA and their contemporaries neither lacked influence, nor were entirely devoid of wider appeal—although usually only on specific issues—whilst an examination of their ideology, as below, shows that it was driven by more than a reductive 'cultural atavism'.[15] Indeed, SCAPA's appeals to

10 Elizabeth Waterhouse writing in *A Beautiful World*, 1 (1893), p. 2.

11 *The Auckland Star*, 30 June 1894, p. 4.

12 LMA/A/SCA/04/003.

13 Peter Mandler, 'Against "Englishness": English Culture and the Limits of Rural Nostalgia, 1850–1940', *Transactions of the Royal Historical Society* 7 (1997), pp. 155–175.

14 Matless, *Landscape and Englishness* (London, 1998), p. 25.

15 Readman, *Preserving the English Landscape*.

preserve the countryside and urban environments from spectacular advertising were made, like those who built art galleries and public parks, on the basis of their utility to and the rights of the general population to sites of leisure, well-being and betterment.[16] As I examine below, they were also made through a developing language of regulation and 'amenity' that hinted at developing contemporary approaches to the expert management and planning of urban and rural spaces that had more in common with the CPRE's approach than has perhaps been allowed.[17]

There is, nevertheless, no doubt that SCAPA were broadly part of the preservationist movement and indeed they shared correspondence and objectives with both the CPS and National Trust, and later the CPRE. In their foundational essay the question of what the society stood for did include much that was aesthetic and framed issues of advertising control in terms of threats to either beautiful landscapes or historic buildings. Indeed, in later years, as we shall see, their focus moved almost entirely towards the countryside and architecturally valuable sites, although this was a move perhaps tinged with pragmatism after many bruising encounters with trade bodies and parliament. At the core of SCAPA's opposition to advertising there certainly appears to have been something of a streak of nationalism that argued for the protection of landscapes and historical buildings which were bound up with notions of British identity. Advertising near Westminster Abbey a 'church dear to all men of English blood, consecrated by history as well as religion, and in architectural glory of supreme excellence' was thus an 'affront to practical intelligence', whilst the Provost of Edinburgh was urged to prevent the growth in eye-catching signage on Princes Street or it would 'not long be the Mecca of romantic students' and Sir Walter Scott himself' should 'renounce the rock' from beyond the grave.[18] Yet there was also a profoundly communal flavour encoded in a concept of national value founded on the rights of

[16] Hazel Conway, *People's Parks: The Design and Development of Victorian Parks in Britain* (Cambridge, 1991); Helen Meller, 'Urban Renewal and Citizenship: The Quality of Life in British Cities, 1890–1990', *Urban History* 22:1 (1995), pp. 63–84.

[17] Elizabeth Baigent, '"God's Earth Will Be Sacred": Religion, Theology, and the Open Space Movement in Victorian England', *Rural History* 22:1 (2011), pp. 31–58; Ben Weinstein, 'Questioning a Late Victorian "Dyad": Preservationism, Demolitionism and the City of London Churches, 1860–1904', *Journal of British Studies* 53:2 (2014), pp. 400–425.

[18] Evans, *The Age of Disfigurement*, pp. 60–61.

all citizens to enjoy beautiful environments. 'Taste' Evans argued 'is not confined to one class…the simplicity of the rural prospect is a portion of the national wealth which it is empathically a popular interest to save from destruction and impairment'.[19]

It was, nevertheless, the preservation of architectural beauty in and around Princes Street in Edinburgh that provided the first notable success for opponents of outdoor advertising—at least in legislative terms—since the various prohibitions on sky signs at the start of the 1890s. SCAPA had gathered sufficient support and momentum from its inception to promote private bills in parliament in 1893 and in 1894, but both failed to gain enough support. Legislation was, however, never SCAPA's only plan of attack; a consistent campaign of letter writing to local authorities, MPs and newspapers was the hallmark of their activism. Between 1894 and 1895, for example, they were one of a number of active voices that succeeded in urging the Office of Works to stop the 'desecration of Nelson's Column' by advertisers who projected their slogans onto the national monument.[20] In 1897 they secured the removal of the 'monster lettering' from the Shot Tower near Waterloo Bridge amongst other small successes.[21] These early successes focused on emblematic locations and on particularly large or unusual forms of advertising rather than simple posters or more mundane locations, but were rather piecemeal in nature. When opposition to large-scale advertising in Edinburgh spilled into the newspapers it thus provided the opportunity to test the appetite for legislative remedies.

In 1895 there was considerable comment in the press about advertisements for 'drugs' and 'fluid beef' which 'extend in gigantic letters along the side of the lower part of Calton Hill and which catch the unwilling eye'.[22] Accordingly, in 1896 the Edinburgh Corporation applied for unprecedented powers to control and licence where advertisements might be sited in the city, but this was rejected by parliament.[23] Their resolve

[19] Richardson Evans, 'Advertising as a Trespass on the Public', *The Nineteenth Century* 37:220 (1895), pp. 968–980 (p. 969).

[20] *Sheffield Telegraph*, 25 April 1895, p. 2.

[21] *London Evening Standard*, 6 September 1897, p. 6; *A Beautiful World* 9 (1903), p. 8.

[22] *The Scotsman*, 15 June 1895, p. 12.

[23] *A Beautiful World*, 8 (1899), p. 12.

was further hardened in 1897 by attempts to erect an illuminated sign for Bovril on James Court overlooking Princes Street, a proposal that the Lord Provost, anticipating a 'storm of indignation' from the citizens, argued would 'interfere with the quiet repose of what is perhaps the finest city view in Europe'.[24] Although Bovril complied with a request from the Provost to reconsider, as the manufacturer themselves pointed out, other signs were being erected in similar locations. The continuing spectacle of advertising in such a treasured site of civic pride and Scottish identity meant the Corporation felt it unwise to rely on the goodwill of other advertisers who might show less sensitivity about public outcry.[25] Accompanied by outraged coverage in the press, when the Corporation returned to a legislative solution in 1899, they found that the current parliament looked more favourably upon the request.

The Town Clerk recorded that 'the principle is that the Corporation, representing the community shall have the right to say where such advertisements may be put, and of course to prevent them being placed where the amenity of the city may be injured'.[26] In making their case for enhanced powers Edinburgh Corporation lent specifically on this right of citizens to have their representatives prevent 'offensive placards disfiguring the City without regard to local interests'. They argued they should be trusted to 'control and regulate' what constituted an 'eyesore or injury to amenity' because they represented local opinion, unlike the advertising companies who typically came from outside Scotland. 'A new growth' they reasoned 'like the evil in its present magnitude, requires a new remedy'.[27] The exceptional outcome of the Edinburgh case owes much to a perception that the city was a unique and nationally important architectural treasure, a sentiment that campaigners and the press were able to martial to their advantage. The importance of the case for this study, however, lies in the allying of the term 'amenity' to notions of popular consent to imply a meaning beyond mere historical and architectural beauty. Whilst also framing corporation desires in a language of popular rhetoric, amenity was here invoked to underscore the value of

[24] *Edinburgh Evening News*, 20 December 1897, p. 2.

[25] This is an extract from the presentation of the Edinburgh Corporation to the select committee considering their bill, reproduced in *A Beautiful World* 8, p. 15.

[26] Ibid.

[27] Ibid.

protecting urban space for its experiential qualities and utility to the population. Indeed, this understanding of amenity, expanded upon later in this chapter, would become perhaps the defining feature of not only outdoor advertising control, but the way the British state came to conceive of the relationship between the environment, public rights and experience.

For Edinburgh Corporation, amenity appears to have been more than just a subjective judgement about pleasantness, implying that visual delight had an experiential quality that had certain function as part of modern life. Nevertheless, the powers awarded to Edinburgh were exceedingly rare in this period and were only replicated in one other instance. In the summer of 1900 the Quaker company erected two very large advertisements for their oats on the cliffs at Dover, causing immediate consternation in the local corporation.[28] The disquiet over the 'Dover Cliff Desecration', as one paper had it, swiftly captured the attention of the national news.[29] By November a letter in which an undersigned list of lords, ladies, clergymen, architects and academics 'interested as all Englishmen are in the fair fame of Dover' protested the outrage was presented to the Mayor and Town Council, although they were already taking action.[30] As in Edinburgh the case presented an opportunity for SCAPA to make their case for tighter control, though they were more prominent in the press on this occasion. The *St James's Gazette*, in thanking SCAPA for taking action to bring the 'abominations' to the attention of the public, argued that 'the Dover cliffs are chosen [by Quaker] because they meet the eye of every traveller to or from our shores and the sentiments of those who feel the beauty that dignity or the pathos of the scene according to their mood are brutally outraged and disregarded'.[31] As the framing of these responses suggests, the Dover cliffs scandal was inflamed not by the damage it did to the town, but, as Readman noted, quoting from the local paper, because it defaced 'the white cliffs of Albion'. If Edinburgh, the Athens of the North had made its case clothed in the national importance of preserving the city's beauty, in Dover the white cliffs were presented as a timeless

[28] *Whitstable Times and Herne Bay Herald*, 14 July 1900, p. 2.

[29] *St James's Gazette*, 8 November 1900, p. 6.

[30] *Dover Express*, 20 November 1900, p. 5.

[31] *St James's Gazette*, 21 November, p. 4.

natural 'symbol of the island home which an Englishman loves so well'.[32] Nevertheless, the efforts of the local authorities, SCAPA and even the billposters' associations themselves—who recognised the damage done to their reputation and the danger of trend-setting legislation—to persuade the American company to remove the signs voluntarily, fell on deaf ears.[33] As a result, the *Dover Corporation Act* was proposed and adopted in short order conferring similar powers to Edinburgh. The local advertising interests, perhaps recognising the damage already done by proxy to their reputation, choose not to contest the bill.[34]

It was assumed by the billposters that the approval of the Edinburgh and Dover acts held the potential to set a dangerous precedent. Both acts were exceptionally wide ranging, covering all manner of advertisements and allowing only limited time before existing hoardings and advertising stations would need to be re-licenced. Indeed, it was the perennial fear of the trade that any system of licencing would immediately lead to the extinction of their businesses at the hands of local authorities. Bill-posting company owner David Allan, speaking to the House of Commons committee considering the Edinburgh bill, had argued that the passing of that act would be 'disastrous to the bill-posting trade… it would be almost impossible to carry on', whilst J.O Rogers, chair of the United Billposters Association (UBA), argued that 'the business in Edinburgh would be destroyed'.[35] That this was and remains an unfounded fear can be confirmed by any reader simply by noting the amount of billboards and illuminated signs still in use in the twenty-first century. Moreover, in the early part of the twentieth century, as this chapter argues, in reality there was little credible threat of regulation becoming suppression. The approval of the Dover and Edinburgh bills did, nevertheless, expose the desires of local authorities to generate greater regulatory powers over outdoor advertisements and anticipate the pattern of opposition to these desires from billposting companies.

In the two years running up to the Dover scandal around thirty local authorities from all across Britain and Ireland proposed clauses that

[32] *Dover Standard*, 24 August 1901, p. 5 quoted in Readman, 'The Place of the Past in English Culture', p. 206.

[33] Sheldon, *The History of Poster Advertising*, pp. 102–104.

[34] Ibid., p. 153.

[35] *The Scotsman*, 20 April 1899, p. 7.

broadly followed the idea of licencing any hoarding or structure used for advertising, whilst some unsuccessfully tried to add walls and frames. Indeed, even before the Edinburgh bill was passed, in 1899 Loughborough Corporation's bill requested the powers to licence all hoardings and structures, which was reduced through negotiation to a prohibition on all boards over 12 feet in height.[36] In the following years preceding the passage of the 1907 *ARA* at least 68 of the bills promoted by local authorities contained similar clauses, which were objected to by the various trade bodies and members of parliament, who allowed nothing stronger than restrictions on billboards above 12 feet in height.[37] Indeed, even after the 1907 *ARA* the form of the byelaws framed under it still roughly followed this idea: that the most acceptable compromise between commercial interests and local government control was to restrict the height of the apparatus used for advertising and that blanket licencing would not be allowed.[38] The importance of this settlement is what virtually none of the bills and byelaws *did* include though. Very few contained a prohibition on any kind of legally displayed posters. Indeed, even the Edinburgh and Dover cases had shown little concern for posters per se—although the final bills did contain controls over posters and frames on walls—not least since the type of disordered bill sticking practices were already covered by the long-standing forms of legislation covered in Chapter 2 and had not ceased. The Edinburgh outcry had ensued from large, illuminated signs and letters in a historic and architecturally valuable location, in Dover the outcry had been against giant hoardings in front of emblematic landscape features. There was little discussion of posters at all. Indeed, even SCAPA were quite clear in several instances that their objective was 'spectacular advertising'—although quite what constituted such was vaguely defined. So long as postering was ordered, limited in amount and did not deface areas with high amenity then they wished only for them to be moderated and controlled. In 1890 Evans, who was nevertheless clear that he disliked all posters and signs as a rule, argued 'I am not arguing against posters as posters [and] ...no one dreams of banishing

36 *Leicester Chronicle*, 4 March 1899, p. 5.

37 Most of the clauses are individual sections in Corporation's general powers acts and similar, so they are hard to track. The number is based on Cyril Sheldon's exhaustive list compiled in 1937. Sheldon, *A History of Poster Advertising*, pp. 146–168.

38 It would not be until the *Liverpool Corporation Act* in 1930 that powers similar to the Edinburgh or Dover Acts would be entertained again, see Chapter 5.

them…the proposition for which I claim assent is that if license in spectacular advertising takes forms or reaches dimensions which constitute a public evil, it is the veriest claptrap to object to authoritative interference on the ground that trade is thereby hampered'.[39]

Though the billposters might characterise SCAPA as 'the Society of Busybodies' and dismiss them as 'cranks and faddists, the possessors of ample leisure' their ideas—particularly that the most workable solution lay in extensive local licencing powers—tallied with the efforts of an increasing number of decidedly practical local authorities.[40] In 1903, for example, attempts by local corporations to pass private bills containing advertising restrictions had become so common that *The Billposters Journal* stated that 'the annual legislation campaign' cost the UBA £2000 per year.[41] Although the trade lobby, as SCAPA noted in the same year, tended to claim a great deal more agency than they really had, since many bills failed on opposition from ratepayers or parliament to other clauses.[42] Regardless, the modification and dismissal of the great majority of the clauses—usually to the 12 feet rule, typically referred to as either the Halifax or Farnworth models after the towns in which they were first applied—certainly suggests some influence was being exerted by the outdoor advertising industry lobby.

The general similarities of the clauses proposed, the standardisation of the amendments made and the two occasions where corporations were allowed to gain genuine powers of licencing give us a general picture of the different positions of each party at the start of the century. Local corporations wished to establish the potential to control what went where and tended to base their appeals for licencing powers on the ability to enforce standards of safety (over dangerously large and unstable hoardings) or to curtail the most egregious examples of advertising excess. Posters, for the most part, appear to have been an accepted part of the urban environment so long as they were orderly. This was also broadly SCAPA's position, who had maintained from their inception that they

[39] Evans, *The Age of Disfigurement*, p. 32.

[40] *A Beautiful World* 1, p. 11 and 8, p. 30.

[41] Quoted in *A Beautiful World* 9, p. 31.

[42] *A Beautiful World* 9, p. 11.

desired a 'law by which the local representative authorities will be empowered to regulate public displays of advertising notices of all kinds'.[43] Central government favoured uniformity in statutory powers but, like the advertisers and billposting companies, they wished to avoid too severe a set of restrictions on commercial freedom and the rights of private property owners. What all parts of government agreed upon, as did the various trade organisations was that the central issue was the reigning in of advertisements that disfigured valuable landscapes. As the billposting associations made clear to SCAPA in 1903: they agreed in the 'propriety of restraining disfiguring displays…other than posters' and did not dispute that advertisements in certain locations were to be condemned. However, they felt these cases were so rare that they 'did not justify any general adoption of authoritative control'.[44] The Edinburgh and Dover cases had achieved the latitude they had because it had been easy to make the case that disfigurement was occurring when historic or nationally symbolic environments were threatened by such spectacular displays. For the majority of local authorities though, without being able to demonstrate either a groundswell of support or an outrageous example of advertising excess, the powers they could garner were severely curtailed.

Amenity and the First Advertising Regulation Acts

In 1902 a memorandum from the Home Office and Local Government Board disallowing a clause from Leamington Corporation on the Dover model expressed the opinion that these types of powers should only be approved in cases of proven necessity.[45] Necessity, though, was very restrictively defined. Even when an outcry or necessity might be shown, the system of bringing clauses for control into corporations' general bills meant, as SCAPA pointed out, that gaining the types of powers that they and local authorities wished to promote relied on the confluence of sufficient provocation with an opportune moment to promote a private bill. If this principle was held to, SCAPA argued, 'places in which exactly the same provocation exists [as Dover and Edinburgh] are cut off from the

[43] Evans, *The Age of Disfigurement*, p. 40.

[44] *A Beautiful World* 9, p. 34.

[45] *A Beautiful World* 8 (1903), p. 30.

chance of redress, unless they happen at the same time to need Parliamentary powers for other purposes'.[46] Conversely, where no outcry existed, the clauses were disallowed or restricted to the Farnworth and Halifax models. Against this background there was a recognition that it might be favourable to create a framework for the creation of general byelaws by local corporations. After attempts in 1904, 1905 and 1906 the *ARA* became law in 1907, the passage of which was facilitated by negotiations to make the bill acceptable to all parties between SCAPA and the billposters associations.[47] During the passage of the bill there was, nevertheless, some rankling in parliament that followed the familiar debate over commercial freedom and the value of landscape protection. Future Prime Minister of Northern Ireland James Craig asked whether 'firms who advertised [were] to be interfered with simply on the sentimental ground that their announcements were exhibited in a manner which interfered with the beauty of the landscape[?] Were the sentimentalists in a county council to have it in their power on the whim of the moment to ruin a whole industry?'[48] William Moore, in contrast, argued that the bill represented a good start on the general principle that 'local bodies should have complete control of all advertisements', whilst Evelyn Cecil offered the opinion that 'if the beauty of the country was to be retained the sooner they dealt with the matter the better' as 'he shuddered to think what would happen to the Lake District' if advertising like that recently seen at Niagara Falls were to be allowed.[49]

The Act was, for a number of reasons rather flawed in the eyes of organisations like SCAPA, but it also ushered in a number of important concepts. As was the case with a great deal of legislation of the period it was merely permissive in nature, allowing local authorities to make byelaws in two instances. The first section simply reproduced what had been agreed in so many instances: that corporations and councils might control hoardings and similar structures used for advertising over 12 feet high, echoing similar provisions already included in the *Burgh*

[46] Ibid.

[47] Hansard, HC, 14 June 1907, vol. 176, cc. 28; Sheldon. *A History of Poster Advertising*, pp. 168–169 mentions the importance of the pre-legislative negotiations.

[48] Ibid., cc. 20–21.

[49] Ibid., cc. 22 and 29.

Police (Scotland) Act 1903.[50] The second section reflected the preoccupation with the protection of areas of countryside and parks that were sites of leisure, allowing byelaws that restricted advertisements that 'affect injuriously the amenities of a public park or pleasure promenade, or …disfigure the natural beauty of a landscape'.[51] The significance of this part of the law was that it brought to the fore both the importance of protecting certain valuable landscapes and encoded the concept of 'amenity' in laws that governed certain spaces. Although it had been applied with similar meaning in the Edinburgh debates, it would begin to appear with increasing regularity, particularly in the 1907 *ARA's* better known cousin the 1909 *Housing, Town Planning etc. Act (HTPA)*. This act, too, was permissive, allowing local authorities to prepare town planning schemes 'with the general object of securing proper sanitary conditions, amenity and convenience', indeed several local authorities would attempt to use this designation (and similar in subsequent town planning acts) to prohibit advertisements in planning schemes, without much success.[52] What these laws and those that followed did do though was introduce amenity as a concept that would 'become a reference point for town planners thereafter' and the key battleground in outdoor advertising control.[53]

Although the term amenity had existed in law for some time, it had, and to a certain degree still has, a nebulous use. As planning historian Phillip Booth argued, amenity is a term that is defined in British law principally by custom and usage, not by strict definition; professionals recognise amenity when they see it, yet defining it in the abstract is, perhaps deliberately, challenging. Amenity thus justifies intervention in

[50] *Advertisements Regulation Act*, 1907 (7 Edw. 7. c. 27), s. 2 (1); *Burgh Police (Scotland) Act*, 1903 (3 Edw. 7. c. 33).

[51] Ibid., s. 2 (2).

[52] *Housing, Town Planning etc. Act, 1909* (9 Edw. 7. c. 44), s. 59 (2) for example in 1926 the Minister of Health indicated to Oxford that the restrictions on advertising included in their town planning scheme should not be included. Sheldon, *A History of Poster Advertising*, p. 178.

[53] Philip Booth, *Planning by Consent: The Origins and Nature of British Development Control* (London, 2003), p. 61.

the development of land whilst concealing the actual reasons for the interference.[54] It appears to have been used relatively little in English law before the end of the nineteenth century, although it is made considerable use of in Scotland from at least the 1820s to refer to the pleasant characteristics of use and usefulness in private property. In Scotland in the mid-nineteenth century amenity might, for instance, be one of the characteristics of a private home or garden, alongside notions like privacy and comfort, or be a value that might be prejudiced by the proposed construction near to residential property of a 'coal gas manufactory'.[55] Ornamental plantations might 'greatly enhance the amenity' of General John Hamilton's mansion on the Dalzell Estate or, most often, it was a characteristic protected in acts that granted powers to use or acquire land and natural resources near existing property.[56] With its great vagueness, it spoke to a longer lineage of Scottish law that allowed the owners of private property to protect their rights and usage of land against damaging ingressions.[57] It does not appear to have been used with any frequency with these meanings in English law until the later part of the nineteenth century, but then fell into common use with a similar sense.[58]

Scotland also forged ahead in lending amenity an association with the urban picturesque and the historical. In 1875 the Cockburn Association, one of the key advocates of the Edinburgh Act in 1899, was formed 'for the preservation and improvement of the amenity of Edinburgh and its neighbourhood, specifically focused on preserving the city's natural and historic beauty', Cockburn himself having been no lover of the modern or

[54] Philip Booth, 'The Control of Discretion: Planning and the Common-Law Tradition', *Planning Theory* 6:2 (2007), pp. 127–145 (p. 140).

[55] House of Commons Papers, Twenty-Sixth Report of the Commissioners for Making and Maintaining the Caledonian Canal, 13 July 1830, 668, vol. 15 VX.111, p. 4; Journals of the House of Commons (1688–1834), 21 May 1827, 8 Geo IV, vol. 82, p. 477.

[56] An Act for vesting and securing the Lands of Muirhouse in the County of Lanark in General John Hamilton of Dalzell, 1833 (3 William IV, c. 6), Schedule (B); *Bill to Facilitate Drainage of Lands in Scotland*, 1847 (10 Vict. c. 11), s. 10.

[57] Richard Rodger, 'The Evolution of Scottish Town Planning', in George Gordon and Brian Dicks, *Scottish Urban History* (Aberdeen, 1983), pp. 71–91 (pp. 76–85).

[58] *Bill for Preservation of River Thames Above Teddington Lock for Public Recreation, and for Regulating Pleasure Traffic*, 1884 is the earliest this study could find; *Railway Fires Act*, 1905 (5 Edw 7. c. 11), s. 2(3) stipulates that a railway company pay compensation to the owner of any land who suffers loss of amenity as a result of a fire that the railway extinguishes.

the purely functional aspects of the urban.[59] Yet amenity here is a rather passive idea rooted in historical and aesthetic notion of architectural value. It is Elgin, fourteen years later, that gives us a hint of the direction of travel of the idea of amenity. In 1889 the draft rules of the Elgin Amenity Association stated:

> The Objects of the Association are the preservation and improvement of the natural attractions of Elgin and its neighbourhood, the encouragement of efforts for the promotion of the means of healthy and elevating recreation for its inhabitants and generally the promotion of the amenity of the city.[60]

Like the Cockburn Association and many others that were springing into existence around Britain and Ireland their objectives centred on the picturesque and historical and involved raising money for beautification projects, but they also invoked an association between these aspects of the urban environment and the health, leisure and general well-being of the inhabitants. In an era where public parks, libraries and art galleries were being placed at the heart of concepts of citizenship, the gradual adoption of the language of amenity was encoded with a profoundly positive and active relationship between space, citizenship and the population's well-being.[61]

Amenity thus spoke to the objectives of opponents of outdoor advertising, for whom controlling signs and hoardings was not purely a question of protecting the aesthetically delightful, at least in the beginning of the movement. In SCAPA's founding essay, Evans argued that:

> There is, I repeat, no reason under the sun why the places where human beings work or dwell should be repulsive. The cottages, the inns, the homesteads that delight the eye of the traveller in rural districts were not constructed with any deliberate regard to picturesque effect...The old

[59] W Forbes Gray, 'Letters of Some Old Scots Jurists', *Juridical Review* 36:4 (1924), pp. 322–338 (p. 335): Rebecca Madgin and Richard Rodger, 'Inspiring Capital? Deconstructing Myths and Reconstructing Urban Environments, Edinburgh, 1860–2010', *Urban History* 40:2 (2013), pp. 507–529.

[60] *Elgin Courant, and Morayshire Advertiser*, 20 August 1889, p. 4.

[61] Meller, 'Urban Renewal and Citizenship'; Anglea Loxham, 'The Uses and Abuses of Public Space: Urban Governance, Social Order and Resistance, Avenham Park, Preston c.1850–1901', *Journal of Historical Sociology* 26:4 (2013), pp. 552–575.

> courts, with their grim, smoke-encrusted tenements of plain brick, soothe the sense simply because no jarring addition has been allowed.[62]

The term amenity was, as the same time, being used to describe a certain usefulness derived from ordinariness in residential districts. In Newcastle in January 1895 a group of ratepayers objected to a hoarding, which by secluding a space near two walls was creating an area in which immoral behaviour was taking palace 'greatly tend[ed] to the lowering of the amenity of a respectable residential district'.[63] This was not, as was so often the case a plea based on visual disorder or disfigurement, but an appeal over the character of a residential area that speaks to the rights of the citizens to 'respectable' lives. In the same year Richardson Evans linked the visual and sometimes physical disorder of uncontrolled advertising with the rights and freedoms of citizens as a national public, arguing that SCAPA was engaged in the 'protection of one of the chief elements in the national wealth; or, to look at the matter, not as a question of collective property, but of individual liberty [we] claim for the seeing eye the same relief from wanton injury as is already afforded in the case of every other organ of the sense'.[64] As Chris Otter has argued, if visuality was the primary sense through which Victorian society encoded ideas of bourgeois civility, advertising threatened the generation of good behaviours because it detracted from the affective nature of beautiful vistas and organised, civilised space.[65]

Quite why amenity, both as a term descriptive of pleasantness and utility and, importantly, as legal term started to see more frequent usage at this point is challenging to pin down. In 1896 the term was sufficiently ubiquitous in its association with urban improvement schemes that one opponent of amenity societies derided 'amenityists' for their influence on private property and the expense and fuss they caused to gain 'the privilege of walking over a few score yards of wet grass alongside a dirty stream…while there was a good decent road'.[66] For the most

[62] Evans, *The Age of Disfigurement*, p. 15.

[63] LMA/A/SCA/05/004/020, 'Proceedings of the Newcastle Council, Quarterly Meeting', 6 February 1893, pp. 195–197.

[64] Evans, 'Advertising as a Trespass on the Public', p. 968.

[65] Chris Otter, 'Making Liberalism Durable: Vision and Civility in the Late Victorian City', *Social History* 27:1 (2002), pp. 1–15.

[66] *Elgin Courant, and Morayshire Advertiser*, 4 February 1896, p. 5.

part, though, amenity was broadly depicted in a more positive light. The important transition in its usage in legal discourse appears to have been a change from a notion of rights of useful pleasantness in private property, to a similar application over public space. In the 1907 and 1909 Acts it implies something resembling a public right or perhaps a municipal duty to preserve pleasant architecture and landscapes as a common good. In 1903 SCAPA, in conference with billposters, stated that their purpose was not the banning of postering, but 'preventing such displays [of advertising] as the average opinion of average people would pronounce to be inconsistent with the amenities of a given spot'.[67] The usage of amenity here was allied with a vaguely egalitarian reliance on the opinions of 'average people'—rather than the views the artists and poets so active in the preservationists movement—but also hinted at how subjective and nebulous the amenity of a 'given spot' could be. As a concept, amenity would come to encompass the qualities that most, if not all locations possessed. However, in the early part of the century its limitations, and thus the limitations of the new laws, were that it was almost exclusively bound-up with a positive notion of beauty or utility that was confined to rural and historic locations.

Rural Beauty and Historic Value

Agreement on the value of the countryside and picturesque landscapes by the early years of the twentieth century was approaching something of a consensus, but the shape of legislation and SCAPA's own materials emphasised that mundane urban environments were of secondary importance. Evans had argued in 1893 that 'whilst nearly all recognised the need to preserve the countryside, too many were ready to condemn the city as inherently ugly'.[68] Indeed, this apparent equal regard for urban environments was reproduced in the SCAPA manifesto which promised 'to promote a regard for dignity and propriety of aspect in towns'.[69] Beyond these pronouncements though—whether because of a membership that drew heavily on a certain aesthetic elite or through simple pragmatism—SCAPA's most successful campaigns dealt with rural beauty

[67] *A Beautiful World* 9, p. 34.

[68] Evans, *The Age of Disfigurement*, pp. 60–61.

[69] LMA/A/SCA 01 and 02 have multiple examples of this.

and historic buildings. Indeed, their priorities reflected the tone of both legislation and patterns of outdoor advertising control before the Second World War, which did very little to alter the amount of poster advertising in urban areas or challenge the perceptions of the amenity of extant urban spaces. If, as the billposters argued in 1903, that there was little in London worth protecting, then the decision of all but two of the major firms by 1905 to cease erecting large signs in the countryside demonstrated the broad acceptance that there was some inherent value in protecting rural areas.[70]

There is little doubt that, as had been the case in Dover and Edinburgh this regard for the rural and historic was tied up with national identity. Indeed, as historians have demonstrated, contemporary interest in the countryside was particularly flavoured in England by the articulation of national identities tied to a rural idyll.[71] Although, as has subsequently been argued the contemporary influence and importance of these cultural productions might be questioned, there was a clear sense that the countryside was productive of both Englishness and healthy English bodies.[72] Nevertheless, questions of the ways it might be preserved were complicated with notions of Conservative and Unionist ideas of private property, the Liberal propensity towards national land reform and the emergence of socialism.[73] Yet, whilst undoubtedly rooted in these nationalist ideals, outdoor advertising control was also part of a decidedly international network of shared ideas concerned not only with national identity, but the purpose and experience of various environments. Acknowledging the

[70] Moran, *The Business of Advertising*, p. 121.

[71] Martin Wiener's *English Culture and the Decline of the Industrial Spirit* (Cambridge, 1981) was arguably the foundational examination of this. Also: David Corbett, Ysanne Holt and Fiona Russell (eds), *The Geographies of Englishness: Landscape and the National Past 1880–1940* (New Haven, 2002); Georgina Boyes, *The Imagined Village: Culture, Ideology and the English Folk Revival* (Manchester, 1993); Alun Howkins, 'The Discovery of Rural England', in Robert Colls and Philip Dodd (eds), *Englishness: Politics and Culture 1880–1920* (London, 1986), pp. 160–202.

[72] Peter Mandler's 'Against Englishness' took issue with Wiener's argument. Alun Howkins, *The Death of Rural England: A Social History of the Countryside Since 1900* (London, 2003), pp. 25–26 discusses the way the rural was imagined as a producer of good, English health.

[73] Paul Readman, 'The Edwardian Land Question', in Mathew Cregoe and Paul Readman (eds), *The Land Question in Britain, 1750–1950* (Basingstoke, 2010), pp. 181–200 (p. 183).

international context of their activities shows movements like SCAPA as instrumental in framing the negotiation between urbanisation, modernity and fledging notions of national heritage across the industrialised world. The English or British attachment to rural life and the landscape was hardly unique, but then neither were SCAPA acting in isolation. Correspondence in their files shows a network of international organisations exchanging information about legislation and measures taken in different countries in North America, in Europe, especially France, Germany, Switzerland and Italy, as well as Japan.

In 1903 SCAPA spoke glowingly of their correspondence with Prussian and Hessian preservationists on the passing of a law that allowed local authorities to prohibit the display of 'advertising boards, notices or pictorial devices as disfigure the landscape'. The concept that governed protection of land must, proponents of the legislation argued, be the 'higher utility' of the landscape, to tourists and to 'town people' who travelled for 'recreative pleasure'. It was the sacred duty of [their] generation …to preserve for posterity these beautiful tracts of the Fatherland'.[74] Similarly, legislation presented for the consideration of the *Conseil d'Etat* the *Société pour la Protection des Paysages de France* (French Society for the Protection of Landscape) echoed the sentiment that the natural beauty of France was a national treasure that nourished patriotism and culture, but which was interfered with by constantly multiplying posters.[75] In 1912, having spoken at the first international congress of the *Bund Heimatschutz* (a German landscape preservation society) in Paris, Evans was invited to the second via the suggestion of the English branch of the League for the Preservation of Swiss Scenery.[76] Correspondence from the City of Chicago in 1901 shows SCAPA requesting copies of and news on the progress of legislation to control advertising stations,

[74] *A Beautiful World* 9, pp. 40–43.

[75] Ibid., p. 51.

[76] LMA/LMA/A/SCA/03/002/010 'Europe', Letter to Evans from *Geschaftsstelle des Bundes Heimatschutz*, 26 April 1912. *Heimat* and thus *Heimatschutz* are slightly challenging to translate directly. The letter to Evans offers 'German League for the Preservation of Scenery', but *Heimatschutz* implies both the protection of the environment in a physical manner and a sense of local character, which was coming into tension with German nationalism, thanks to Sheona Davies for helping with this translation. See: Celia Applegate, *A Nation of Provincials: The German Idea of Heimat* (Berkeley, 1990); Alon Confino, *The Nation as a Local Metaphor: Württemberg, Imperial Germany and National Memory 1871–1918* (London, 1997).

but which indicates the exceptional difficulty of interfering with private property in the USA.[77] Correspondence with a number of American cities and states, the American Civic Association, as well as a request for information from a member of the House Assembly in Bermuda, indicate a variety of legislative and regulatory strategies being discussed, as well as the seemingly limitless energy of Evans as a letter writer.[78]

Japan was at the forefront of what would become 'heritage' protection laws in the late nineteenth century and the passing of laws governing outdoor advertising in 1911 was received enthusiastically by SCAPA.[79] If advertising was an intrinsically modern aspect of the visual environment, it followed that it could no more have a place on or in proximity to historically and architecturally valuable buildings than it did in the culturally significant rural landscapes. In Japan, as SCAPA noted, in 1914 the application of the *Law for Advertisements* of 1911 meant that police in Tokyo had issued an edict that all outdoor advertising near imperial palaces, residences and graveyards, as well as in the grounds of temples and shrines must be removed in three months.[80] The 1907 *ARA*, they lamented, did not come close to matching these kinds of powers. Influenced by what they saw as the success of both the Japanese laws and similar French legislation, SCAPA had considerable hopes for what became the 1913 *Ancient Monuments Consolidation and Amendment Act*, but were disappointed when the act simply extended the provisions of the 1907 Act to allow local authorities to prohibit advertisements that would damage the amenities of ancient monuments.[81] This was another layer of welcome advertising control, but it did not go far enough for SCAPA who had

[77] LMA/A/SCA/03/002/001, Letter to Evans from City of Chicago Council Chamber, 9 January 1901.

[78] LMA/A/SCA/03/002/001, Various correspondence labelled 'America' c.1901–1911.

[79] Hannah M. Szczepanowska, *Conservation of Cultural Heritage: Key Principles and Approaches* (London, 2013), p. 97.

[80] LMA/A/SCA/03/009/014, Correspondence from George Geoffrey Dawson, editor of *The Times*, quoting a letter from Yokohama, 30 May 1914. See: Geoffrey R. Scott, 'The Cultural Property Laws of Japan: Social, Political, and Legal Influences', *Washington Law Journal* 12:2 (2003), pp. 314–401.

[81] *Ancient Monuments Consolidation and Amendment* Act 1913 (3 and 4 Geo 5 c. 32), s. 19.

pushed for the legislation to include a clause that, like French legislation, prohibited advertisements in a defined radius around monuments.[82]

Yet, with hindsight the 1913 Act was more important for SCAPA's cause than they might have allowed at the time. As prolific writer on the topography and buildings of England Edmund Vale declared, it represented the means 'whereby the state admitted a cultural responsibility towards its own history never before assumed by the British government'.[83] What it did was signal that historical value was the domain of the state, but also showed a wider confluence of certain ways of looking at spatial value that echoed the approaches in the 1907 *ARA* and the 1909 *HTPA*. For the moment, this was only hinted at, as the Act was still very much concerned with ancient sites and uninhabited buildings, but it did draw together a number of crucial ideas about public interest and ownership, national identity, amenity and the material environment, whilst considering the process of seeing and governing those spaces that betokened the development of more comprehensive approaches to spatial governance. Section thirteen, like its predecessor from 1900, allowed the public a right of access to any monument taken over by the local authority. In sections six and twelve it introduced the idea of 'national importance', positioning public access and, in section twenty-two 'public interest' as aspects of the environment to be judged and managed by the state. Moreover, section eighteen allowed the relaxation of local byelaws to facilitate 'the erection of buildings of a style of architecture in harmony with other buildings of artistic merit existing in the locality'. Considered alongside the ability to restrict advertisements in section nineteen, the 1913 Act placed ideas of historic value and public interest into the sphere of the fledging discipline of planning. The importance here though is that reading it against the 1907 *ARA* and 1909 *HTPA*, we can see the character of a system that considered the experience and a certain sense of public, utilitarian value in the environment to be worthy of legislation and protection.

The problem with the legislative process, at least for those who wished to establish greater regulation of advertising, was that the emerging interpretation of amenity and public interest and where these qualities might

82 LMA/A/SCA/01/001 SCAPA Minute Book 1911–1922, 12 November 1912.

83 Edmund Vale, *Ancient England: A Review of Monuments and Remains in Public Care and Ownership* (Malvern Wells, 1941), p. 4.

be found were highly subjective and, at least in this period, proving frustratingly narrow. SCAPA had, upon the passing of the 1907 *ARA*, urged local authorities to make acts under the new law, proposing an ambitious model byelaw of their own.[84] In largely rural areas there was initially some doubt about the precision of terminology necessary to prohibit advertisements under the 1907 *ARA*. Lindsey County Council, Lincolnshire, for example, had proposed a byelaw that would schedule the whole county in 1910 but had been rebuffed by the secretary of state who believed that any bill must specify specific landscapes to be protected. SCAPA offered the opinion that the spirit of the law was that all clearly rural landscapes, not merely certain attractive ones were to be protected from advertisements and it was this view that ultimately won out. Amenity, in this instance, was something that was held to be present in broad terms in all rural landscapes. In 1912, following the success of Hampshire in obtaining a blanket prohibition, Lindsey secured such a byelaw.[85] By 1914 SCAPA listed 25 counties who had made such byelaws, but where rural and urban areas overlapped, they proved more difficult to enact successfully and only 29 borough and urban districts had done so at the same point.[86]

As SCAPA themselves allowed, the numbers of corporations who could not or saw no point in producing byelaws exposed the deficiencies of the 1907 *ARA*.[87] County authorities that administered almost entirely rural areas were by the 1910s as a matter of course being allowed to effectively ban all advertising hoardings and stations, should they so choose, based on the general perception that rural landscapes were inherently disfigured by the various erections used for advertising. However, authorities with mixed urban, village and rural areas could not make blanket laws and found it understandably challenging to frame laws that made specific reference to all areas that they thought should be covered. Indeed, even where local authorities that governed villages and urban areas specified beauty spots, the interpretation of what precisely constituted an injury to

[84] LMA/A/SCA/03/002 series 'Correspondence with Local Authorities' shows a comprehensive letter-writing campaign to local authorities urging them to adopt SCAPA's proposals.

[85] LMA/A/SCA/03/002/017, Correspondence with Local Authorities 'L', Lindsey County Council, 1912.

[86] LMA/A/SCA/03/009/014, Byelaws sanctioned, c. August 1914.

[87] LMA/A/SCA/03/009/014, Letter from Evans to Sir George Younger M.P, 24 April 1913.

amenity was rarely in their favour. Hastings, for example, had specified six beauty spots in the town, and when an electric sign was erected that was visible from one of these spots, they took the case to court under the 1907 *ARA*. However, the magistrates dismissed the case because they concluded that simply being visible from the beauty spot did not automatically mean the same as injuring amenity in the way the 1907 act was framed.[88]

Against the challenges of accurately anticipating the interpretation of the laws any impetus for greater powers seems to have petered-out somewhat and the usage of the 1907 *ARA* did not meet the hopes of SCAPA. Between 1913 and the end of the 1920s there was little change in character of laws governing outdoor advertising. More stringent bills were still promoted by SCAPA and their supporters, but blocked in 1913 and—with a cessation for the First World War—1919, 1920 and 1921. Viscount Birkenhead, the Lord Chancellor, exemplified the tone of the opposition in parliament in the 1910s and 1920s when he 'overwhelmed with ridicule' several proposed advertising bills, arguing that more potent planning legislation was both 'futile and unnecessary' and imposed 'upon local authorities jurisdiction which they do not seek, which they have never asked for, and which they will undoubtedly judging by the experience of the last few years, fail to use when they have obtained it'.[89] In debating the 1920 bill in the Lords, Lords Onslow and Southwark too argued that there was little need for more extensive powers when the existing ones were not used to their fullest extent.[90]

Pitched against this opposition to further powers, and despite Evans' insistence on the urban and rural nature of SCAPA's objectives, the direction of opposition to outdoor advertising from both the society and the state turned squarely towards the picturesque and the historical. In promoting the ultimately successful 1925 *ARA* Earl De La Warr summed up this position when he asked:

> ...whether we, as a civilised people, really care for beauty, whether we intend to permit individuals actuated purely by commercial motives to

[88] *Hastings and St Leonards Observer*, 17 October 1936, p. 16.

[89] Hansard, HL 19 May 1922, vol. 50, cc. 525.

[90] Ibid., cc. 518–520.

> vulgarise the natural beauties of our countryside, and to plaster the vicinity of our public buildings with their abominations.[91]

In a report to the committee Evans argued that, whilst the society had as much regard for:

> The street of workingmen's cottages in the suburb of a manufacturing town as well as a mountain pass in the Highlands …effort must be confined to the immediately practicable: that the cases in which the public opinion was already right for action must come first.

He added that 'each little triumph in this kind or that detail is was felt would do something to raise the standard of ordinary thought'.[92] Small triumphs were for Evans and SCAPA part of the process of changing the direction of opinion about advertisements in an environment where legislative progress had ground to a halt. Throughout the period, though, SCAPA maintained a campaign of promoting their cause in the newspapers and letter writing to local authorities. In their correspondence they encouraged greater use of the 1907 ARA, but also suggested to local authorities that they insert clauses into their agreements to rent their own properties prohibiting advertisements. The results were largely positive with significant property owners like Bath and Blackpool confirming they did precisely this, the latter commenting that they did so as the 1907 *ARA* was 'scarcely applicable to the requirements of Blackpool'.[93] In contrast, some smaller authorities, like Bury in Lancashire, held too little property to think this would have any real impact.[94] Evans also looked for further small victories by targeting the aesthetic elite from which the billposters were so fond of alleging SCAPA's support came. Throughout 1912, for example, Evans wrote to the wealthiest Oxford colleges asking them to support his campaign by prohibiting advertisements on the considerable amount of property which they owned,

[91] Hansard, HL 4 March 1924, vol. 56, cc. 481.

[92] LMA/A/SCA/01/003 'Report to SCAPA Committee and Members' by Evans, 5th February 1910, p. 1.

[93] LMA/A/SCA/03/002/005, Letter from Town Clerk of Bath, 10 February 1914; Letter from Country Borough of Blackpool, 11 February 1914.

[94] LMA/A/SCA/03/002/005, Letter from Town Clerk of Bury, 2 April 1914.

Fig. 4.1 Advertising and signs on a petrol station and chemist, unknown location, 1935 (*Source* SCAPA Files LMA/A/SCA/06/002/005, reproduced with the permission of the CPRE, © CPRE)

receiving a number of affirmative responses as well as words of support for SCAPA's position.[95]

SCAPA's non-legislative campaigning was perhaps most successful in building upon a general consensus that led to an eventual reduction in roadside advertising (Figs. 4.1, 4.2 and 4.3 for some later examples that SCAPA took action against). Naturally, many of the issues of roadside advertising touched upon questions of protecting rural landscapes or pleasure areas, but eliminating roadside signs was complicated by the inconsistency of the byelaws passed by local authorities and the amount of

[95] LMA/A/SCA/01/001 SCAPA Minute Book 1911–1922 for example minutes from October 1912. On landholdings see: David Spencer, 'Pulling Out of Colleges and Landed Property: The Oxford Colleges and the Church Commissioners', *Area* 32:3 (2000), pp. 297–306; J.P.D, Dunbabin, 'Finances Since 1914', in Bryan Harrison (ed), *The History of the University of Oxford. Volume VIII: The Twentieth Century* (Oxford, 2004), pp. 639–682.

The amount of property owned by Oxford colleges is not clear, but in 1873 the Cleveland Commission reported that they owned 185,000 acres of land, although this had fallen to 127,690 acres by 1989.

Fig. 4.2 Roadside Hoardings, Cathays Park, Cardiff, 1938 (*Source* SCAPA Files LMA/ A/SCA/06/002/005, reproduced with the permission of the CPRE, © CPRE)

Fig. 4.3 Roadside and Gable Advertising, White Mare, Pool Bridge, Sunderland, 1937 (*Source* SCAPA Files LMA/ A/SCA/06/002/005, reproduced with the permission of the CPRE, © CPRE)

apparently rural areas that fell into locations governed by mixed or urban authorities. SCAPA's strategy was to target the advertising companies, support individual complaints and seek the support of other interested societies and parties. In 1910 Evans wrote to as many of the motoring publications as possible, asking for their support in opposing roadside advertisements. He argued that pressure could be effectively put on the tyre, oil and vehicle manufacturers, who were the main advertisers on roadsides, because their success relied upon country driving remaining 'an escape from ugliness and worry'. 'England' Evans continued 'offers far and away the most attractive ground for picturesque travel on wheels. But if the benighted competition of the motor manufacturers in making the roadside hideous is allowed to go on, the lover of the unspoilt scenery will be driven across the seas'.[96] In 1912 he wrote to the Royal Automobile Club and Scottish Automobile Club, urging them to put pressure on local authorities to pass byelaws under the 1907 *ARA*.[97] Indeed, SCAPA were writing to a sympathetic audience; at a meeting of their executive committee the previous month the Scottish society had decided to use their influence to promote the adoption of byelaws by county councils.[98] Moreover, support for SCAPAs position in the newspapers anticipated their strategy. Lauding the reputedly unique charms of the English village, one correspondent in Leamington argued that 'we must do all we can to save the villages [from] ... the degradation of the staring advertisement' before adding that 'if the advertisers could be persuaded to remove them, they would suffer no less'.[99]

The success in encouraging public opinion and motivating enthusiasts was illustrated when in 1913, having initially rejected SCAPAs 1910 request to cease roadside advertising Michelin alongside the other major tyre manufacturers agreed to cease. Writing to SCAPA, they explained they would be placing stories in newspapers to the effect that not only were they removing thousands of their signs from roadsides, but would

96 LMA/A/SCA/03/009/009 Letter to "Automobilist" Journals from SCAPA, 7 September 1910.

97 LMA/A/SCA/01/001 Minute Book 1911–1922, 20 February 1912.

98 *Aberdeen Free Press and Journal*, 8 January 1912, p. 2.

99 *Leamington Spa Courier*, 16 August 1912, p. 7.

also remove any signs upon receiving objections from the public.[100] In the same year British Petroleum agreed to reduce their roadside advertisements, although Evans was unsuccessful in his request for them to cease advertising on urban streets, and by 1927 Shell Oil—formally a heavy investor in roadside billboards and long-time hold-out—announced it would remove all signs except those at its petrol stations and which displayed prices.[101]

The process of curtailing motoring-related advertisements eliminated only part of the multitude of advertisements on roadsides, and as the above images from SCAPA's files show, issues of roadside advertising persisted as did SCAPA's campaigns against them until after the Second World War. Nevertheless, the campaign against motor advertising illustrates both the success of SCAPA's non-legislative tactics and the broad agreement by the 1920s that rural and picturesque scenery needed protection from disfiguring elements. Indeed, so complete was the perception that extra-urban roadsides should be kept as clear as possible that in the 1928 *Petroleum Consolidation Act*—promoted with considerable support from the newly created CPRE—section 23 allowed local corporations to make byelaws prohibiting or regulating the appearance of filling stations to preserve 'the public the amenities' of any rural scenery, place of beauty or historic interest, public park or pleasure promenade or any 'street or place which is of interest by reason of its picturesque character' including the view of or from that place. This last element was of vital importance because of the way it expanded the definition of how amenity functioned to a wider notion of how a whole area was experienced.

The importance of this act, then, is in illustrating the evolving definition of how amenity was being applied by the 1920s. In 1925, having failed in their previous proposals, SCAPA were instrumental in negotiating with advertising trade representatives to facilitate the passage of the 1925 *ARA*, which extended the provisions of section two of the 1907 act to clearly include scenic elements of roads, rail or waterways, all villages

[100] For example: *Oxfordshire Weekly News*, 2 April 1913, p. 8 carried the story. Also: LMA/A/SCA/03/009/009.

[101] Terry Nevett, *Advertising in Britain: A History* (London, 1982), p. 161. Shell's decision was made, according to Speakman, upon the realisation that it was just as effective to simply advertise on the sides of their own vehicles. Malcolm V. Speakman, *Shell's England: Corporate Patronage and English Art in Shell Posters of the 1930s* (Unpublished PhD Thesis, University of Manchester 2014).

as well as historic buildings and urban areas of outstanding beauty.[102] This version of the act, however, merely extended the definitions of the types of places to which the 1907 law applied and thus lagged behind the *Petroleum Consolidation Act's* view of amenity in an important way. This piece of legislation saw amenity as something that involved a more holistic, experiential view of an area. It placed people in that area, rather than defining the view of it in a limited manner. The 1907 and 1925 *ARAs* might protect the amenity of a specific place, but from the 1920s other acts were beginning to absorb a language of amenity and environmental value that increasingly borrowed from the art of planning. These interwar acts—the *Ancient Monuments Act* in 1931, the 1923 *Housing, &c. Act* and the 1932 *T&CPA*—are discussed in the following chapter and articulate new ideas about the management and experience of lived spaces. The creation of this body of legislation, flawed though it would prove to be, bound-up control of outdoor advertising with the newly emerging processes of town planning and further deepened the debate on advertising control as an important factor in the preservation of amenity.

SCAPA's objective, though, by the 1930s had started to drift from the wide rural and urban remit of their original ambitions. The collection of powers to control outdoor advertising that they had helped create had very little scope for the protection of residential, commercial or industrial areas of towns and cities, but material produced by them places little emphasis on expanding the purview of existing laws. SCAPA were not anti-urban, nor simplistically concerned with the preservation of a particular historical period or architectural style. Evans' earliest pronouncements made clear that, whilst SCAPA were avowedly elitist, sometimes paternalistic and certainly preservationists of a sort, they were neither dogmatically opposed to advertising, nor did they disregard the simple experiential qualities of quotidian urban environments. Guided by SCAPA, the 1925 ARA specifically protected the amenities of any area 'frequented by the public on account of its beauty or historic interest', which could include parks and exceptional residential areas.[103] Nevertheless, in the expression of their objectives, it increasingly became clear that SCAPA, whilst having considerable regard for beautiful areas of towns

102 *Advertisements Regulation Act*, 1925 (15 and 16 Geo. 5 c. 68), s1(1) a–c. On SCAPA's role, see Hansard, HL, 04 March 1924, vol. 56, cc. 477–481.

103 *ARA*, 1925, Section 1(1) c.

and cities, by the 1920s saw most urban space as worthy of little in the way of advertising control. In one of 'Evans' last published contributions to the society in 1926, he included only the protection of 'villages in the simple countryside and spots of particular architectural or historical interest in towns' when he talked of the societies objectives. In the same year another pamphlet declared that the society was 'Concerned with advertising only where the display injuriously affects the amenities of outdoor life'.[104] There were certainly mentions of protecting pleasant residential districts, but the scope of SCAPA's objectives had shrunken to match the progress of laws available.

One explanation for the changing focus of SCAPAs direction may be pure pragmatism; as the chapter has argued there was little appetite outside of SCAPA for control of advertising in mundane urban spaces and there was considerable popular impetus behind control in the countryside. SCAPA's change in attitude is also illustrated by their close allying and eventual incorporation into the CPRE after its creation in 1926. Quite understandably, the CPRE had relatively little interest in urban spaces and focused their attention on very detailed and effective campaigns to rid the countryside, particularly rural roadsides, of advertisements. As Oliver Hilliam's study of the relationship between SCAPA and the CPRE has shown, their partnership was instrumental in keeping pressure on government and local authorities, but it coincided with the drifting of SCAPA from their urban objectives.[105] Whether this drift was the cause of their close co-operation or a symptom is not clear. Ultimately, the two organisations' co-operation led to their extensive consultation on the 1947 *Town and Country Planning Act (T&CPA)*, the passing of which the CPRE felt brought 'to an end the long and sustained struggle by the CPRE to arm the public representatives with effective powers to protect the public highway' from outdoor advertising, and 'finally gave councils powers to prohibit advertisements except on sites approved by them'.[106] Of course, as the following chapter argues the 1947 *T&CPA* was far from the end of the story, but SCAPA too echoed the sentiments of their allies: that

[104] British Library (BL)/PP1092bac, 'A Brief Sketch of the SCAPA Aims and Work', 1926, p. 1.

[105] Oliver Hilliam, 'Idea 20: Cutting the Clutter', in Peter Waine and Oliver Hilliam (eds), *22 Ideas That Saved the English Countryside: The Campaign to Protect Rural England* (London, 2016), pp. 186–197.

[106] Ibid., p. 195.

the passing of the act achieved their objectives and that there was little left for them to do.[107]

Conclusion

The 1907 and 1925 *ARA*s and their waning concern for the less aesthetically pleasing aspects of the urban environment meant that by the early 1930s SCAPA had, in legislative terms at least, achieved much of what it set out to do. Local authorities had usable, if flawed powers of control and SCAPA's activism subsequently focused upon attempts to eliminate the small number of remaining signs on rural roads and on pressuring local authorities to use the 1925 *ARA* to object to advertisements that 'interfere[d] with natural beauty'.[108] The association did continue until 1953, but with the death of the previously indefatigable Evans in 1928 and their attempts to expand the laws further largely frustrated, they showed little desire to extend their activism to the wider urban landscape. Pushing for advertising control in towns and cities would, as Chapter 5 shows, be the realm of the local authorities themselves. Indeed, whilst the 1932 and more importantly the 1947 *T&CPAs* were the starting points for local corporations' attempts to exert greater control over advertising, SCAPA concluded in 1951 that the 1947 Act finally achieved all they wanted in legislative terms. Though they would maintain a vocal presence in debates, by the post-war they were mostly a spent force whose objectives increasingly resembled those of their counterparts the CPRE.[109]

There is, though, little doubt SCAPA had proved effective in promoting a subjective definition of how advertising should be controlled, and they left a legacy of laws on which future legislation would be built. Moreover, their combination of tactics had drastically, although not entirely, reduced advertising in rural areas. Their activism had also been part of a wider change that enshrined the notion of amenity in law and in public discourse in a manner that would be fundamental to the future of advertising control and definitions of what urban space and the

[107] LMA/A/SCA/01/004, 'Committee Minutes', 21 November 1951.

[108] 'Ugly Signs and Posters', *The Times*, 8 January 1930, p. 8; 'The SCAPA Society Annual Report', *The Times*, 12 June 1931, p. 13.

[109] In 1951 SCAPA considered winding down and transferring funds and members to the CPRE, and there are no records of further independent meetings after 1952. LMA/A/SCA/01/004, 'Committee Minutes', 21 November 1951.

regulation of it was for. Amenity during this period, whilst never entirely losing its status as a vague definition of pleasantness or aesthetic appreciation of buildings and landscapes, took on a new meaning. As SCAPA themselves argued—and which became ever more obvious through the objectives and tone of a host of laws on ancient monuments, town planning and housing—amenity was beginning to imply citizens' rights to enjoy the benefits of what might be broadly considered public space. Unspoiled rural countryside was a national resource, as were historic monuments, and both had a distinct role to play in producing the healthy bodies and minds of the nation. This development of more holistic views of how space was encountered and experienced, and how such processes might be managed, also betokened the incorporation of the language of town planning into legislation that governed Britain's landscapes. Outdoor advertising was, nevertheless, still relatively unchallenged in towns and cities, where legislation simply did not cover or have the potential to cover mundane and extant urban spaces. As a result, despite a regulatory framework that limited heights of billboards, SCAPA's founding objective—to place regulatory decisions in the hands of local authorities—remained elusive and, at the outbreak of the Second World War looked no closer to being achieved.

CHAPTER 5

Billboards, Planning and Urban Modernism

Abstract This chapter proposes that the driving force behind the advancement of outdoor advertising control after the 1930s were local authorities. It argues that their understanding of 'amenity' demonstrates the pervasive nature of urban modernism and planning to governing towns and cities in the post-war period. The acts of the interwar period could not be used to create order and uniformity in more mundane and extant urban spaces, but in the post-war local corporations utilised the 1947 Town and Country Planning Act to expand the definition of amenity to include any residential areas. Despite staunch opposition from the advertising trade, local corporations were able to persuade central government that it was desirable to protect even the 'meanest' and most dilapidated residential areas against outdoor advertising and did so by depicting a social democratic subject, who had the right to live in spaces uncluttered by the intrusions of commercialism.

Keywords Urban modernism · Planning · Amenity · Post-war · Governmentality · Local government

J. Greenhalgh, *Injurious Vistas: The Control of Outdoor Advertising, Governance and the Shaping of Urban Experience in Britain, 1817–1962*, Palgrave Studies in Economic History,
https://doi.org/10.1007/978-3-030-79018-9_5

In 1909 in the Court of Appeal hearing the case of Nussey vs Provincial Bill Posting Company—a dispute over whether bill-posting might be allowed as part of a contract which prohibited the use of land for 'any noisy, noisome, offensive or dangerous trade'—William Danckwerts, K.C argued that 'it cannot be said of an [advertising] hoarding that it will offend against any sense: the utmost that can be said against it is that it is a blot on the landscape'.[1] Yet, the court, by a majority, disagreed. Lord Justice Buckley declaring that whilst the 'draftsman in using "noisy" and "noisesome" had exhausted offences to the ear and the nose... "offensive" might well be applied to that which offends the eye'.[2] In considering these definitions the case anticipated the challenges of defining what exactly might or might not be offensive to the eye or person, or, as this chapter examines, 'injurious to the amenity' of an urban area. The series of acts that began with the 1907 *ARA* and had continued through the 1920s enshrined the notion of amenity in the law, but whether amenity was something all or few areas possessed, what constituted offence to the eye or did not, and how outdoor advertising should be understood to prejudice or enhance amenity proved challenging to define. The character of legislation and the broad tide of public sentiment agreed that by the 1930s outdoor advertising certainly had a detrimental effect on rural areas and historic buildings. Yet whether amenity existed in the great variety of mundane residential and industrial areas of Britain's cities would be the defining question of the final phase of debates over outdoor advertising regulation.

The chapter proposes that the driving force behind the advancement of outdoor advertising control after the 1930s were local authorities, and that their understanding of amenity demonstrates the pervasive nature of urban modernism and planning to their approach to the towns and cities they governed in the post-war period. It begins with an examination of local authorities' powers at something of an impasse, exploring the practical ways local corporations and councils sought to regulate advertising within the existing frameworks of byelaws, whilst pushing for practical change to elements like rating laws. Local authorities had little desire to eliminate advertising, but as other chapters showed, harboured a distinct

[1] Quoted in BL/PP1092bac 'Advertisement Disfigurement and Law: SCAPA Pamphlet No. 4', October 1929, p. 1 on the case see: 'English Cases', *Canadian Law Journal* 45 (1909), p. 477.

[2] *Solicitor's Journal*, 17 April 1909, p. 424.

desire to have the potential to regulate, tax and order advertising. In this ambition they were largely frustrated by both the limits of the law and the interpretation of it by central government and local magistrates and sheriffs. The second section moves on to study the ways that local corporations, particularly Liverpool gradually framed their ambitions to control advertising as part of larger schemes to regulate urban space that was recognisably based in and facilitated by the discourse of town planning and amenity present in a host of legislation during the period. Amenity, the chapter suggests, is the central concept around which planners and local authorities sought to organise and govern space, but in the years before the war it was interpreted inconsistently, and questions of amenity value usually excluded mundane and extant urban spaces. In the final section the chapter examines the ways that the post-war patterns of urban modernism redefined amenity around the rights of citizens, establishing broad patterns of control for urban corporations and councils by the end of the 1950s. At the heart of this process was the construction of a social-democratic subject, who was envisaged as possessing the rights to the greatest possible dignity in his or her environment, not merely as a consequence of any post-war consensus, but as a form of governance in itself.

Local Regulation at an Impasse

As Chapters 3 and 4 argued, local authorities had been concerned with regulating outdoor advertising by various means since at least the latter part of the nineteenth century. The first phase of advertising controls were enacted in elements of improvement acts or much larger municipal codes and thus they were symptomatic of the emerging regimes of governance that sought order in space and criminalised anything that inhibited the free circulation of people and goods within cities.[3] In the late nineteenth and early twentieth centuries, further forays were made into advertising regulation that sought to secure greater order in the presentation of advertisements and eliminate the most egregious and obstructive examples of billboards and hoardings. By the end of the First World War this meant that broad controls on content and size were established, as well as

[3] Patrick Joyce, *The Rule of Freedom: Liberalism and the Modern City* (London, 2003), p. 88.

some ability to levy rates on advertisements. Nevertheless, only in exceptional cases were local corporations, as we saw in Chapter 4, allowed any more restrictive powers as a matter of course. Whether they achieved greater powers, like Dover and Edinburgh, or had to compromise on their ambitions, the way the legislation was actually operated by local authorities showed little desire to eliminate advertising altogether.

The operation of Edinburgh's extensive powers suggests that regulation and the potential for unchallenged discretion were the Corporation's chief objectives, not elimination. After some early clashes with advertisers, in 1906 Edinburgh Corporation sought to pass an act that would weaken the powers of the Sheriff under appeal and give the Corporation limitless licence to control advertising, but this attempt failed, actually confirming the role of the Sheriff as the final arbiter in disputes.[4] Disagreements with billposters tended to erupt over how far the architectural amenity of the city extended into the outlying districts, but after some testing of the Sheriff's interpretation, the parties established enough of an understanding that between 1920 and 1926 only 18 applications to erect advertising hoardings were refused and only four of these were appealed to the Sheriff. In the inquiry into a proposed consolidation bill of 1926, the billposters themselves suggested that extended powers in the bill were unnecessary since the corporation did not use the ones they already had for 'outlying areas'.[5]

Corporations seem to have understood that there was little appetite at national level for advertising restrictions and were likely not interested in total suppression anyway. Put simply, where advertising stations were maintained and located judiciously, they represented a necessary even desirable part of the economic functioning of their towns and cities. For this reason the issues of taxation and how it might be more effectively levied was a continual aspect of the discourse surrounding advertisements in the first half of the twentieth century. From the 1890s onward, SCAPA believed that one of the most effective ways that advertising might be restricted was a direct tax on poster advertising, pointing to the success of taxation in France following the introduction of a new law in 1911.[6] Supporting this idea the 1901 Royal Commission on Local Taxation also

[4] Cyril Sheldon, *A History of Poster Advertising* (London, 1937), pp. 164–166.

[5] *The Scotsman*, 16 April 1926, p. 10.

[6] Evans, *The Age of Disfigurement*, p. 21.

concluded that 'another form of taxation which can properly be regarded as entirely local and which ought…to be freely put in operation at the option of Local Authorities, is the taxation of posters and similar advertisements'.[7] The Exchequer, however, proved deaf to calls for a tax on posters, ignoring SCAPA's frequent representations on the subject, whilst local authorities focused their attentions elsewhere.

The chief focus of local authorities was remedying the weaknesses of the 1889 *Advertising Stations (Rating) Act (ASRA)* itself. Under conditions where local rates were being brought into sharp focus by the breadth of local authorities' municipal ambitions and thus expenditure, maximising rates revenue was a source of considerable discussion.[8] Until the 1889 *ASRA* made it clearer how posters or hoardings might be rated, local corporations had found rating advertisement hoardings at all a challenge. However, even when this act was passed the definitions of how and what might be rated remained difficult to police. The 1889 *ASRA* allowed a rateable value based on the amount an advertiser or advertising company paid to rent a hoarding or wall. However, it did not rate this separately from the parent hereditament. This meant that whomever the law considered the occupier of, for example, a house with a billboard on the gable, was liable for the total rate for both the house as a dwelling and the value of the billboard. Properties that shared a wall or grounds complicated the situation further and had the overall effect of making it difficult to know what portion of the rates assessment was levied upon the advertising station.[9]

The status quo went against both the impulse of corporations to try and create ever more comprehensive bodies of knowledge, but also the straightforward desire to extract revenue. Indeed, advertising stations represent just one of a host of grey areas that were the subject of widely varying rules and practices in the interwar period. In 1927 a questionnaire from the Central Valuation Committee (CVC)—created under the 1925 *Rating and Valuation Act* for the 'purpose of creating uniformity in valuation for rating'—listed advertising stations alongside woodlands,

[7] Lord Balfour of Burleigh, *Report of the Royal Commission on Local Taxation*, 1901, C.D. 638, p. 71.

[8] See: Avner Offer, *Property and Politics, 1870–1914: Landownership, Law, Ideology and Urban Development in England* (Cambridge, 1981), ch. 18 and 21; Martin Daunton, *Just Taxes: The Politics of Taxation in Britain, 1914–1979* (Cambridge, 2002), ch. 11.

[9] NA HLG/56/1116, LCC letter to the Ministry of Health, 19 January 1931.

sporting rights, petrol pumps and village halls as areas where rating practices needed to be reviewed.[10] In 1932 Plymouth Corporation wrote to the Ministry of Health asking them to consider updating legislation 'so as to remedy the present injustices of rating tenant occupiers of premises in respect of advertisement hoardings attached or adjacent thereto over which that have no control'.[11] The following year the Rating and Assessment Committee of the Association of Municipal Corporations' (AMC) passed a resolution that the law should be amended to rate the advertising stations as separate hereditaments.[12] According to the LCC the defects in the existing law were 'so serious, that in practice the law is not followed and the advertising stations are, as a rule, separately assessed'.[13] When industrial premises were derated or in instances where hoardings and billboards were on farm land they were seldom rated at all, because of a confusion over whether advertisements formed part of the agricultural ratings or buildings themselves.[14] Despite a clarification from the CVC in 1929 that there were circumstances where advertisements on farmland could be rated, officers of the Inland Revenue in 1931 did not rate advertising stations on farmland as a matter of course, whilst rating railway advertising raised too complex a set of issues over ownership to be done effectively.[15]

In the first half of the century corporations and councils promoted byelaws or supported the amendment of legislation like the 1925 *Rating and Valuation Act*, but there was only some progress.[16] In 1932 the LCC's General Powers clause which would have separated advertisements and occupation into separate hereditaments was rejected following staunch opposition from the trade bodies, who believed (likely correctly) that it would increase their costs.[17] It would, however, be a mistake to

[10] *Rating and Valuation Act*, 1925 (15 and 16 Geo. 5 c. 90), s. 57(1). Circular to local authorities reported in *The Scotsman*, 3 June 1927, p. 4.

[11] NA/HLG/56/1116, 'Resolution Passed by the City Council', 29 July 1932.

[12] NA/HLG/56/1116,'Advertisement Hoardings. Rating', 26 October 1933.

[13] NA/HLG/56/1116, LCC letter to the Ministry of Health, 19 January 1931.

[14] *The Field*, 17 Jun 1905, pp. 48–49.

[15] BL/PP1092baa, 'SCAPA Quarterly Papers: New Series No. 2', p. 3; NA/HLG/56/1116. 'Derating Advertising Hoardings', 16 February 1931.

[16] Sheldon, *A History of Poster Advertising*, p. 223.

[17] *The Times*, 14 April 1932, p. 8.

think that local authorities saw rating as an opportunity of and in itself to decrease advertisements per se. Indeed, even in the 1950s when extensive powers to control advertising and rate sites more effectively were finally in place, ministers often criticised their local counterparts for being too lax with advertising licences for their own land, especially where the financial inducement was sufficiently large.[18] Instead, the attempt to create more adequate systems for rating was part of a move to generate more detailed knowledge of that which they governed and by extension create larger, more stable streams of income.[19] Unlike the more holistic priorities of SCAPA and emerging preservationists like the CPRE, these were quotidian problems of local government. They were often dealt with circumstantially, but represented coterminous issues of urban governance and local finance that reflected the interplay and often tensions between the essentially commercial and economic nature of urban space and the job of shaping the lived experience of it.

Taxation, whether a backdoor into regulation that SCAPA thought it would be or not, certainly offered little extra in the way of advertising control. Instead, local authorities continued to work with the 1907 and 1925 *ARAs*, private bills of their own and, occasionally, the various provisions in the acts governing planning schemes, petroleum and ancient monuments. Indeed, when Cyril Sheldon complied an incomplete list of all the local government acts the trade organisations had opposed in parliament or in local government before 1932, he counted over three hundred bills. All of which, barring an exceptional handful discussed below, had been either defeated or amended in line with the broad principles of restricting the height of hoardings and billboards.[20] The various model clauses named after the early century acts of Halifax and Farnworth that only prohibited billboards larger than twelve feet in height, had proved through different iterations, very durable. Naturally, industry standards simply altered to match these standards and these early acts did little to curtail anything but the most excessive forms of advertising in urban areas.[21] Moreover, as the LCC and many others discovered when

[18] NA/HLG/71/1738, Correspondence: G.R. Coles to Street, 2 August 1957.

[19] On the urge to create comprehensive bodies of municipal knowledge, see: Leif Jerram, *Streetlife: The Untold Story of Europe's Twentieth Century* (Oxford, 2010), ch. 5; Joyce, *The Rule of Freedom*, ch. 1 and 2.

[20] Sheldon, *A History of Poster Advertising*, pp. 147–291.

[21] Moran, *The Business of Advertising*, pp. 146–151.

proposing byelaws under the 1907 Act, central government was opposed to the use of the legislation to establish anything resembling a blanket system of billboard licencing in anything but purely rural areas.[22]

Even after 1925, authorities who had a mixture of rural and small urban development found the legislation of limited use when they tried to designate large areas for regulation. The 1925 *ARA* largely solved the issue of creating blanket areas of control for local authorities dotted with villages and even small, picturesque towns—urban districts with fewer than 10,000 inhabitants could not generate legislation of their own—and in 1926 the High Court affirmed the right of county councils to make such byelaws that, in general terms regulated their entire jurisdiction.[23] Nevertheless for authorities with mixed urban and rural areas, the stumbling block remained central government, who often quibbled over the amenity of areas with urban elements. In 1927, for example, Cumberland County Council's proposed byelaws prohibiting advertising without permission across the county were rejected by the Home Office several times because of the mixed quality of various areas. When they were passed, it was in such a watered-down fashion that the Town Clerk complained they did little in reality to prohibit the erection of advertising hoardings.[24] Nor was the only issue the interpretation of Home Office ministers. When local byelaws were passed the definition of amenity was often tested in court, with mixed results. In 1929 when Derbyshire County Council—who had made a byelaw under the 1907 ARA in 1914—brought cases against advertisers for advertising in the small village of Winster, magistrates visited the site and concluded that it definitely damaged the amenities of the landscape, was 'an absolutely eyesore' and commended the Council to 'continue their campaign of putting down these abominable advertisements'.[25] Conversely, in 1931 the county council for Ilkley in Yorkshire took Sheldon's of Leeds to the magistrates over a large sign measuring 157 feet in length that obscured the view of a wooded area. Sheldon's argued that there was little amenity in the area because the board obscured huts and a chicken run and was

[22] NA/HO/45/17318, 'Letter to Hampstead Town Clerk', 27 March 1915.

[23] United Billposting Co. Ltd. V. Somerset County Council, 1926 quoted in NA/HO/45/16607, Home Office Memorandum 176,181/28 15 November 1932, p. 3.

[24] NA/HO/45/16607, Letter from Cumberland County Council, 12 October 1932.

[25] *Sheffield Daily Telegraph*, 28 September 1929, p. 11.

near a sewage works and the magistrates agreed, commenting that the rural scenery was too distant to be affected.[26]

The types of difficulties of passing, enforcing and interpreting the available laws were characteristic of the period and, despite pressure from local corporations, there was little chance to establish systemic forms of licencing or control. Indeed, whilst a desire to establish systems of control is demonstrable in the amount of legislation proposed, one issue was that there was, as yet, little uniformity in local authorities' motivations for greater control. As Councillor L.S. Gumley of Edinburgh pointed out before a select committee considering the 1930 *Liverpool Corporation Bill*, the restriction of 12 feet in height, which most local authorities possessed could hardly have facilitated anything more than public safety, and certainly had little bearing on amenity since it had no restriction on length.[27] Indeed, some local corporations seem not to have considered urban amenity an issue with which outdoor advertising necessarily interfered at all. Rotherham's regional plan of 1925 acknowledged advertisements in rural areas were an aesthetic issue, but framed general issues in more practical terms:

> There can be little controversy as to the need for the control of the many varieties of advertising signs which in certain places are disfiguring the countryside.... of more importance however in the Rotherham Region is the growing tendency to utilize every important road junction for advertisement purposes, so that more legitimate direction boards and distance posts are apt to be missed.[28]

The legibility of signage that guided motorists, not amenity was clearly the issue that most occupied the planners in this instance. Likewise, in nearby Sheffield's 1931 regional plan, advertisements might be 'unmitigated nuisances' in rural beauty spots, but the authors Patrick Abercrombie and T.H. Johnson stated that 'advertisements may be attractive objects in the urban scene'.[29]

26 *Yorkshire Post and Leeds Intelligencer*, 5 September 1931, p. 14.

27 *The Scotsman*, 27 March 1930, p. 8.

28 William Davidge, *The Rotherham Regional Planning Scheme* (Rotherham, 1925), p. 102.

29 Patrick Abercrombie and T.H. Johnson, *Sheffield and District Regional Planning Scheme* (Liverpool, 1931), p. 54.

Urban Modernism, Experience and Public Rights

The 1930s, though, gradually ushered in a period where local authorities' ideas about how to regulate and govern urban space—and thus outdoor advertising—were beginning to coalesce into questions of how both planned and extant spaces might be made more orderly, functional and even beautiful that signalled a change in the language of amenity and outdoor advertisements. In 1930, in an exceptional case, Liverpool managed to gain complete licencing control over all advertisements—except on railways and property owned by the Dock Board—through section 29 of their corporation bill. That this bill was passed into law despite a Home Office report that was averse to it and repeated objections lodged from the British Poster Adverting Association (BPAA) is anomalous in the period, but indicative of the changing discourse of urban governance.[30] Precisely why Liverpool Corporation was able to get section 29 through parliament unmolested is not entirely clear—it narrowly passed objections from multiple interests at committee stage by a vote of four to three and the BPAA had further petitions rejected by the Commons and the Lords—given that similar revisions to the *ARA* proposed in 1928 and 1930 floundered on opposition to extending advertising controls to residential and built-up areas.[31] Nevertheless, the reasoning for this section in the context of the rest of the bill hints at a changing understanding of advertising's role in the environment.

In the Corporation's opinion, the remedies available to them under the existing acts of 1907 and 1925, though adequate to protect the amenity of historic and architecturally valuable areas, were insufficient to control advertising in residential areas and, as result, they had rarely used the available powers.[32] The Corporation also included in their bill provisions that allowed them to repair privately owned working-class dwellings at the landlord's expense if they were neglected and to remove cars forming an

[30] *Liverpool Echo*, 27 March 1930, p. 7.

[31] NA/HLG/54/264, 'Comments on Liverpool Corporation Bill (No. 2), 1930', 28 April 1930; Special report from the Select Committee on Local Legislation, 1929–30, HC Papers, No. 163, Vol. 6, p. 177.

[32] *Liverpool Echo*, 26 March 1930, p. 16; NA/HLG/54/264, 'Supplementary Report of the Secretary of State for the Home Department on the Liverpool Corporation Bill (No. 2), 1930', 28 April 1930.

obstruction in public streets.[33] Taken as a whole, the bill thus contained a rather radical set of ideas about the spatial governance of extant spaces. The extent to which the Corporation sought to interfere in private and commercial property—rather than merely regulate newly created spaces—hints at the emergence of the ambitious ideologies of urban control that characterised the redevelopment of industrial cities in the post-war period. As the *Liverpool Echo* declared this was a bill concerned with 'beautifying Liverpool' and when Mr Raikes K.C., acting for opponents to the bill asked if Liverpool was not a 'rather commonplace commercial city' not only did the newspaper point to Liverpool's fine buildings, it also defended the rights of the whole city to be free from disfigurement. 'Even if Liverpool were a commonplace city, that would be a very strong argument for beautifying it and the Corporation is seeking powers with an eye to the future and in the interests of the community'.[34]

Indeed, it was clear from the Corporation's defence of their bill the manner in which they were considering the disruptive spatial qualities of advertisements as part of holistic understandings of urban governance. T. Peirson Frank, the City Engineer, told the committee that:

> The Corporation had now complete control over the elevations of new buildings and the practical effect of that should not be spoiled by the display of unseemly advertisements in the same street ... In recent years there had been a change in the public view as to preserving rural amenities, but it was even more important to protect suburban areas.[35]

The insistence that residential areas had some intrinsic amenity value to the inhabitants merely as a residential space represents a departure from the dichotomous view of unquestionable rural amenity placed against the unattractive urban. Indeed, Frank's claim inverted the existing logic making the suburban more important, but also imagined control of outdoor advertising a programmatic tool of spatial regulation alongside building controls.

This idea that residential amenity existed as a mere function of being a place people lived was developed in another industrial city too. In 1933,

33 NA/HLG/54/264, 'Draft of Liverpool Corporation Bill (No. 2), 1930', 3 March 1930, sections 60 and 66; *Liverpool Echo*, 25 March 1930, p. 5.

34 *Liverpool Echo*, 26 March 1930, p. 8.

35 Ibid., p. 16.

in support of Salford Corporation's bill, which sought similar powers to Liverpool, Conservative MP for Salford West, Fred Astbury argued:

> The chief opposition to the Bill comes from the billposters...they want to post their bills on every gable-end and on the front of every cottage in the poorer parts of Salford. I say that the poor people in those districts have as much right to protection and to have a pleasurable outlook on life as we have in the better districts...for years these poor people have complained to me that what little outlook they have has been spoiled by these hideous advertisements.[36]

Despite opposing the actual wording of the clause in the bill, Sir Walter Greaves-Lord, Conservative MP for Norwood, nevertheless added:

> Some people think a mean street has no amenities, but I see no reason at all why, because a man lives in a poor house in a poor street, he should have his view defaced by a number of posters, and it seems to me that it is just as much necessary in a mean street to protect the inhabitants of that street from the unlimited exhibition of posters as it is even in the countryside.[37]

Like Liverpool's arguments, this discussion of the bill echoed the growing opinion amongst local authorities that, regardless of the subjective aesthetic appeal of an area, large amounts of any advertising in residential neighbourhoods inured the amenity in a way that was prejudicial to the experience of ordinary life.

The change in language surrounding the control of advertising in the Liverpool and Salford cases reflected a *volte face* in how urban spaces were being understood by certain politicians and local authorities. The purpose of urban governance was being plotted as a tool that had the potential, perhaps even a duty, to preserve as great an amount of dignity in the built environment as was possible as a public right. If no area was too 'mean' to possess some amenity to those who lived there, then it followed that all intrusions into it that did not beautify, like outdoor advertisements, had the potential to demean and degrade. When Sheffield again produced

[36] Hansard, HC, 27 July 1933, vol. 280, cc. 2886.

[37] Ibid., cc. 2901.

a plan for urban redevelopment in 1945, they would plot a course that inverted their previous claims about the amenity of the built environment:

> Our attempt to achieve architectural amenity, however, involves more than the provision of well-designed new buildings. The creation of beauty calls also for the destruction of ugliness, whether it be in existing buildings, advertisements, in flashing signs, in hoarding, in park railing or even in our street lamp-posts.[38]

Amenity derived from the built environment was thus being understood not as merely related to the creation or preservation of the subjectively beautiful, but also being seen in the quotidian railings and streetlamps. Moreover, amenity was something that all areas might have and could be diminished by unsightly elements. Indeed, this was the development of the language of public rights that Evans and SCAPA had bound up with the notion of amenity from the start of the century, but now applied in a manner that assumed some level of amenity in most if perhaps not quite all places. In a 1931 quarterly paper utilising the language of rights bound up in public health legislation, SCAPA asserted that 'it is no more eccentric or highbrowed to object to the uglification of the countryside than to object to a bad smell or distracting noise. The law recognises the title of citizens not only to advertise shoes or sealing wax or to sell petrol but also to enjoy the proper beauties of his native land'.[39] Local authorities were, by the 1930s, extending this logic of public rights beyond the countryside and into the mundane, lived spaces of their cities and towns.

It would be a mistake to think, though that this language reflected a groundswell of support, and there is scant evidence that advertising control was ever of more than passing interest to the public. Newspapers had featured outraged comment from correspondents since the end of the nineteenth century, but advertising control did understandably little to excite genuine public interest. Perhaps outdoor advertising was just too ubiquitous to be noticeable—as SCAPA claimed was the issue in attracting public support—or it could simply have been that citizens perceived other concerns to be more pressing. In 1938 when Mass Observation surveyed public opinion most of the relatively few concerns about outdoor adverting represented the prevailing notion that it was

[38] Sheffield Town Planning Committee, *Sheffield replanned* (Sheffield, 1945), p. 62.

[39] BL/PP1092baa, 'SCAPA Quarterly Papers: New Series No. 3' (1931), pp. 2–3.

a disfigurement to rural areas.[40] When they asked again in 1944 they found that only 14% of people objected to advertising of any sort and an even smaller proportion of this group, mostly middle-class individuals, had specific objections to hoardings as a disfiguring presence in the city.[41]

What was driving corporations desires to control outdoor advertising was, instead, the ideals and strategies of comprehensive redevelopment that emerged in the 1920s and 1930s and showed their greatest expression during thirty or so years following the Second World War.[42] Central to these ideas were the philosophies of development and spatial governance that characterised what historians have called 'urban modernism'.[43] Urban modernism is a term applied to a set of approaches to holistic redevelopment that was characterised by the creation of order and functionality, either through the replanning and creation of new places or the regulation of extant areas. It was expressed in everything from the most ambitious plans for the rebuilding of entire cities to mundane rules governing green spaces or defining clean air and hours of daylight. Most importantly, planners placed the experience of urban spaces at the heart of these processes of regulation and control, arguing that the right sort of environment could have a positive effect on the quality of citizens' well-being, community spirit and ultimately society as a whole.

Urban modernism is usually characterised by the emblematic legacy of architecturally Modernist buildings it has left behind, but these are not our concern here. Instead, the reason that the broad collection of approaches to governance called urban modernism is important is because of how it dealt with already existing spaces, especially those that had

[40] Mass Observation Archive (MOA),'Reactions to Advertising', December 1938.

[41] MOA, 'Public Attitudes to Advertisements', February 1944, p. 5.

[42] Nicholas Bullock, *Building the Post-war World: Modern Architecture and Reconstruction in Britain* (London, 2002); Gordon Cherry, *Cities and Plans: The Shaping of Urban Britain in the Nineteenth and Twentieth Centuries* (London, 1988); John Gold, *The Practice of Modernism: Modern Architects and Urban Transformation, 1954–1972* (London, 2007); Otto Saumarez Smith, *Boom Cities: Architect Planners and the Politics of Radical Urban Renewal in 1960s Britain* (Oxford, 2019); John Stevenson, 'Planners' Moon? The Second World War and the Planning Movement', in H.L. Smith (ed), *War and Social Change: British Society in the Second World* (Manchester, 1986), pp. 58–77 (pp. 59–60).

[43] Simon Gunn, 'The Rise and Fall of British Urban Modernism: Planning Bradford, Circa 1945–1970', *Journal of British Studies* 49:4 (2010), pp. 849–869; Guy Ortolano, Thatcher's *Progress: From Social Democracy to Market Liberalism Through an English New Town* (Cambridge, 2019), p. 20.

no immediate prospect of redevelopment. Urban modernism *did* create gleaming new estates and shopping centres, but most urban spaces could or would not be rebuilt. Urban modernism thus also concerned itself with the mundane, but vitally important ways of controlling these extant environments. This was a quiet radicalism expressed in aggressive control of building height, rigid zoning, smoke abatement laws, the regulation of the shape and colour of doors and windows, defined in expectations of maintained gardens and driveways, all monitored through inspection and planning control.[44] In that sense, it had much in common with the regimes of inspection and sanitation that characterised the late nineteenth and early twentieth centuries, but added more layers. The notion that bound this accumulation of small regulations and controls together was not merely public health or nuisance, it was not just an association between order and functionality, nor was it merely the still-legible traces of liberal governmentality that plotted urban regulation as a spatial technology to produce 'direct moral self-control'.[45] Urban modernism, in relation to outdoor advertising and other elements that injured amenity, expressed the notion that maintaining or even generating feelings of dignity, local identity and pride through an ordered and pleasant environment was itself a technique of governance. Outdoor advertising, like bad smells or noise, disrupted not just some bourgeois civility, but a more basic potential for people to feel dignity in their environment because it was an uncontrolled, unplanned and decidedly commercial aspect in residential spaces.[46] If outdoor advertising could be said to disrupt the amenity—the useful public value of pleasantness or enjoyment—of a landscape, a historic building or an architectural treasure, then the assumption that there were lived spaces in which it was allowed implied that there was no amenity to be had.

This way of viewing how urban space should be governed and shaped was reflected in and encouraged by the creation of a group laws that I touched upon in the last chapter. The 1923 *Housing &c. Act* enabled local authorities to create schemes to preserve 'areas' with 'special architectural, historic or artistic interest attaching to a locality' with 'a view

[44] James Greenhalgh, *Reconstructing Modernity: Space, Power and Governance in mid-Twentieth Century British Cities* (Manchester, 2018).

[45] Joyce, *The Rule of Freedom*, particularly pp. 86–90.

[46] Baker, 'Public Sites Versus Public Sights', pp. 1187–1213; Iveson, 'Branded Cities', pp. 151–174.

to preserving the existing character' which included the 'area prescribing the space about buildings'.[47] The coverage of the 1923 Act indicated a change in direction from the earlier laws, which had tended to be interpreted as restricting protective legislation to the building itself or view of it in a narrow manner. Instead, this view of amenity places citizens in the spaces and asks how they experience the area within a broader spatial and experiential context. Similar ideas of the character of an area or locality were included in the 1925 *Town Planning Act*, whilst the 1932 *T&CPA* allowed the restriction of outdoor advertising in new and extant areas zoned under a planning scheme where the 'amenity' of the locality might be prejudiced by billboards and posters.[48] The 1931 *Ancient Monument Act*, in a similar spirit, allowed for the creation of special areas to 'preserve the amenities' of any ancient monument by restricting development in the 'locality'.[49]

In basic form the view of locality in these pieces of legislation indicates the evolution of ways of thinking about urban experience and the important function the character of whole areas might have, vaguely defined though locality, character and amenity might be. These acts held the possibility of creating whole areas where the visual appearance could be strictly regulated and, expanding the previous provisions for ancient monuments in 1913, carried the seeds of what would become 'conservation areas' and the notion that would eventually emerge in 'heritage setting'.[50] Under these rules, it gradually became an accepted norm that advertisements in close proximity to historic buildings and monuments would not be tolerated. In 1939, describing 'disfiguring advertisements' near Lincoln's Roman Gate the Lincoln-Lindsey Town Clerk encapsulated the development of this orthodoxy, arguing that 'it would be difficult to find a more striking example of undesirable advertisements' (e.g. Fig. 5.1) in such a clearly historic location.[51] Each of these pieces of

[47] *Housing Act*, 1923 (13 and 14. Geo. 5, c. 24), s. 23.

[48] *Town Planning Act*, 1925 (15 and 16 Geo. 5, c. 16), s. 1(2); *Town and Country Planning Act*, 1932 (22 and 23 Geo. 5. c. 48).

[49] *Ancient Monuments Act*, 1931 (21 and 22 Geo. 5. c. 16).

[50] For definitions see: Historic England, *The Setting of Heritage Assets* (2nd edition), online resource https://historicengland.org.uk/images-books/publications/gpa3-setting-of-heritage-assets/heag180-gpa3-setting-heritage-assets/ accessed 20 December 2020.

[51] LMA/A/SCA/06/002/005, Correspondence between Scorer and SCAPA, 6 March 1939.

Fig. 5.1 Newport Arch, Lincoln c.1939 (*Source* SCAPA Files LMA/A/SCA/06/002/005 Reproduced with the Permission of the CPRE, © CPRE)

legislation built on the concept of amenity and refined it, enshrining it as notion that encapsulated the public value of spaces. If the earliest expressions of amenity, discussed in Chapter 4 had seen it as expressing a usage value located in the positive pleasantness of private property, by the 1930s it had taken on a new meaning. It had become enmeshed with the gaze of the planner to imply the rights of the public to enjoy the benefits of environments that were as pleasant as the state could possibly make or, more importantly here, keep them. Nevertheless, during the interwar period, this emerging planning framework remained focused upon aesthetically pleasing areas because of the way local authorities' understanding, or perhaps ambitions for the definition of amenity tended to clash with the prevailing views of the arbiters of the law.

The issue of only being able to protect specially designated areas was brought to the fore when Arthur Evans MP for Cardiff South stood to defend a clause to licence outdoor advertisements in Cardiff's 1934 corporation bill. Evans told the Commons that the Corporation wished:

> To control and regulate, or prevent if necessary, advertisements on private houses occupying a street not within the T&CPA of 1932…The Cardiff Corporation consider it is logical that the people resident in those areas should have the same amenities and protection as the people who are resident within an area under the T&CPA 1932.[52]

The limited amount of any authority's jurisdiction that could be covered by the *T&CPA* 1932 was not the only issue, either. Though the 1932 Act seemed to contain powers to regulate advertising at local level, it proved to be ineffective because of the way it was interpreted. The framing of the law meant that courts had to adjudicate on disputes over amenity between advertisers and local government. In these instances, judgements frequently fell on the side of the advertisers because the judiciary tended to see little amenity value in ordinary urban areas.[53] Even where judgements did go the way of local authorities, the inconsistency of interpretation discouraged widespread uptake. In July 1938 the Harrow Billposting Company successfully appealed against Ealing Town Council claiming that the area in which the Council sought to protect injury to amenity was unaffected by the addition of hoardings. Despite testimony from local residents that the advertisements had a negative effect on a residential area, the magistrates could see no 'serious affect' upon amenities.[54] Yet eight months earlier, despite similar arguments the same appellants had been ordered to remove hoardings where the magistrates sided with the Council, pointing out that that the disputed location was a residential area and the Council did allow outdoor advertising nearby in a designated commercial area.[55]

Even in areas where slightly different laws held sway, for example in Glasgow where outdoor advertising was interpreted under a local act of 1937, the interpretation of amenity was a cause of frustration. In 1938, the local Sheriff sustained appeals by billposters to erect a sign on a gable-end because upon inspecting the residential site he 'found no amenity which could in any reasonable sense be affected…unless one adopted the extreme view' that merely using the site for advertising 'created an

[52] Hansard, HC, 14 February 1934, vol. 285, cc. 2017.

[53] *T&CPA*, 1932, s. 47(1), as noted in Barry Cullingworth and Vincent Nadin (eds.), *Town and Country Planning in the UK* (London, 2002), p. 144.

[54] *West Middlesex Gazette*, 16 July 1938, p. 9.

[55] *West Middlesex Gazette*, 27 November 1937, p. 11.

amenity, the existence of which had hitherto been unsuspected'.[56] The problem with amenity was not merely that there were questions over how to define how much an area had, but whether anywhere had intrinsic amenity at all. In 1934, the Sheriff of Aberdeen held that refusal to licence a hoarding on the grounds of injuring amenity alone, without establishing the nature of the amenity and how it was injured, was contrary to the town planning scheme made by Aberdeen County Council in 1933.[57] In both Glasgow and Aberdeen, amenity was being interpreted as something that described a basic level of pleasantness or beauty, but which could not be presumed to exist in everything. In comparison, in a case concerning the Lancashire village of Galgate in 1939, the opposite was held to be the case. Barrister W.G. Morris, speaking on behalf of billposting firms, argued that the County Council had to 'prove these hoardings constituted a disfigurement of [that] amenity. Amenities could not spring up in three years as the hoardings were not a disfigurement in 1936'. In a less urban setting than Glasgow or Aberdeen, the court disagreed with this premise and fined the firms £1 for each case.[58]

The challenge of defining and interpreting amenity was thus becoming the centre of an ideological conflict that expressed local authorities' ambitions as planners and shapers of urban space. Amenity was a frustratingly nebulous term and though the laws of the interwar period had seemingly created considerable potential for the control of outdoor advertisements, the vagaries of the definitions did not keep pace with how local authorities saw the purpose of urban spaces. Advertising companies and billposters clung to the notion that there was a clear dichotomy between areas with or without amenity. Alongside the majority of magistrates, they positioned amenity as an active notion of beauty or at least pleasantness, whilst local authorities plotted it as a quality present everywhere in some quantity. The latter view cast posters and billboards as automatically deleterious to amenity however artistic or orderly they were. This did not automatically mean outdoor advertising was intolerable—as Ealing Council pointed out, there were spaces where it was suitable—but by the 1930s corporations and councils were increasingly deeming residential areas as entirely unsuitable for advertisements.

[56] *The Scotsman*, 25 October 1938, p. 6.

[57] *The Scotsman*, 9 November 1934, p. 6.

[58] *Lancaster Guardian*, 4 August 1939, p. 5.

Post-war Planning and Local Control

'Amenity', or more likely 'amenities', are probably familiar words to most readers, although, as the past two chapters have argued, the words have a long and somewhat diffuse lineage in legal terms. Amenity as it tends to be used in the twenty-first century usually refers to shops, public transport, parks or anything in certain areas that is broadly useful to the population in the fulfilment of their various needs. Local councils build, fund and encourage the provision of amenities through a variety of strategies and are criticised when shops are too distant, buses are infrequent or local leisure facilities are misused or neglected. However, in the middle of the twentieth century amenity in town planning legislation had taken on a prominent, legally significant, but vague meaning. It was being interpreted as anything 'from an essentially negative restriction against nuisances to a distinctly positive notion of visual delight'.[59] Although amenity meant little more than 'a quality of pleasantness in the physical environment', its centrality as a definition to so much legislation meant that it became the central objective of planners in the post-war period.[60] In addition, because of amenity's nebulous qualities, as Katrina Navickas demonstrates in arguments over rural landscape preservation during the 1950s, debates were often settled by the ability of interested groups to successfully map a host of different meanings onto the word.[61] Shaping whether amenity meant economic function, beauty or merely regulated order had considerable potential to influence what would or would not be allowed in any given space.

If the interwar period had been characterised by a mixture of possibility and disappointment for advocates of greater regulation, then the 1947 *Town and Country Planning Act* would ultimately swing the pendulum of advertising control towards local authorities. However, the initial period of its operation was fraught with difficulties over how to interpret its provisions. The new act, Lewis Silkin, the Minister of Town and Country Planning, promised would contain 'the almost complete prohibition of all

[59] Donald L. Foley, 'British Town Planning: One Ideolodgy or Three?', *The British Journal of Sociology* 11:3 (1960), pp. 211–231 (p. 220). Also: Philip Booth, 'Planning and the Rule of Law', *Planning Theory and Practice* 17:3 (2016), pp. 344–360 (pp. 354–356).

[60] Foley, 'British Town Planning', p. 220.

[61] Katrina Navickas, 'Conflicts of Power, Landscape and Amenity in Debates over the British Super Grid in the 1950s', *Rural History* 30:1 (2019), pp. 87–103.

forms of outdoor advertising in certain specified areas'.[62] In practice the act allowed local authorities to create areas of special control—including all new developments—to refuse permission for any advertisement that prejudiced amenity, and—in what would prove to be a crucial addition—made the Minister the final point of appeal for disputes.[63] What might be areas of special control were limited by the act to 'either rural areas or areas other than rural areas which appear to the Minister to require special protection on grounds of amenity'.[64] Ministerial adjudication, which might otherwise have been a mere footnote, was thus crucial for two reasons. First, because the only areas in which local authorities could not wield arbitrary control of outdoor advertisements after 1947—the extant, unplanned areas that made up the core of most urban areas—were the exact type of locations where amenity value might be contested by advertisers. Secondly, because, with no real prospect of genuinely holistic rebuilding of cities possible during the shortages of the decade following the war, local authorities' desire to regulate their towns and cities fell specifically on these very types of location.[65] Advertisers' and billposting companies seemingly recognised the potential for conflict in this system and unsuccessfully pushed to retain a version of the role the courts fulfilled in the 1932 legislation.[66] Silkin, however, rejected these concerns, issuing what would prove to be the portentous assurance to advertising companies that 'no minister would deal unfairly with any future judgements'.[67]

[62] *The Scotsman*, 30 January 1947, p. 5.

[63] NA/HLG/71/1045, 'Town and County Planning Bill 'B'', 17.1.1, clause 28, undated c. January 1947.

[64] *Town and Country Planning Act*, 1947 (10 and 11 Geo. 6, c. 51), s. 31(3).

[65] On the difficulties of immediate post-war redevelopment see: Junuchi Hasegawa, *Replanning the Blitzed City Centre: A Comparative Study of Bristol, Coventry and Southampton* (Buckingham, 1992); Peter J. Larkham, 'Thomas Sharp and the Post-war Replanning of Chichester: Conflict, Confusion and Delay', *Planning Perspectives* 24:1 (2009), pp. 51–75; Nick Tiratsoo, 'The Reconstruction of Blitzed British Cities, 1945–55: Myths and Reality', *Contemporary British History* 14:1 (2000), pp. 27–44.

[66] NA/HLG/71/1045 'Meeting with representatives of the Scottish poster advertising industry', 21 February 1947; 'Control of advertisements: fourth meeting of committee "A"', 27 March 1947.

[67] NA/HLG/71/1045, 'Draft of speech to the British Poster Advertising Association' by Silkin, 17 June 1947.

It is unsurprising, given their past activism that upon the passing of the 1947 *T&CPA* local authorities immediately tested the extent to which they might stretch the definitions in the new laws.[68] In September 1948, only a month after the new act came into force, Manchester Corporation refused permission for a gable-end billboard in a slum-clearance area, stating that they had 'always striven to avoid gable-end advertisements, which [we] considered to be definitely detrimental, especially to the amenities of a residential area'. They furthermore stressed that this test case was of considerable importance, especially given the inadequacy of the 1932 legislation.[69] Outdoor advertising company Arthur Maiden disputed the amenity of 'one of the poorer neighbourhoods of Manchester', adding that 'the erection of an advertising position, such as we desire, would improve the amenity of this area', whilst the Corporation suggested that the allowing of gable-end advertisements would hasten the decay of a pleasant, if poor residential area.[70] The Ministry, describing the area as 'clearly a working-class district …[of] drab coloured brickwork which has not become enlivened by years of exposure to the Manchester atmosphere', ruled in favour of the advertisers.[71] Indeed, Silkin made public his feelings about where his opinion lay in these disputes, stating that if 'there is any doubt we give the applicant [the advertiser] the benefit of the doubt'.[72]

Manchester's contention that gable-end advertising tended to hasten decay in areas where it became prevalent was echoed by other local authorities. Gateshead, Bolton and 'certain other northern towns' were also flagged by the Ministry in 1950 for having a 'concerning' policy that sought to entirely ban advertising on gable ends.[73] This form of advertising was often painted-on and thus difficult to remove—as the number

[68] The relevant section dealing with the role of the Minister in deciding outdoor advertising appeals appears in regulation 20(4) of the *Town and Country Planning (Control of Advertising) Regulations* (S.I. 1948 No. 1613) that was appended to the original *T&CPA* 1947.

[69] NA/HLG/79/421 'Appeal Hearing', 26 January 1949, p. 2.

[70] NA/HLG/79/421 'Letter to the MoT&CP', 19 November 1948; 'Letter to Arthur Maiden Ltd from Town Clerk', 9 November 1948.

[71] NA/HLG/79/421, 'Appeal Hearing', 26 January 1949, p. 2.

[72] 'Silkin Tells Sign Men of Outdoor Law Clean-Up', *World's Press News and Advertisers' Review*, 31 March 1949, p. 4.

[73] NA/HLG/71/1723, Note ref:1129/30/4-9, 22 February 1950, p. 2.

of 'ghost signs' still in existence will attest—was most common in residential areas and had been a particular nuisance to those using the 1907 acts and its successors as it was not a separate erection to the house on which it was displayed. In 1950 the AMC requested that the Ministry reconsider its position that gable-end advertising 'of a reasonable size [was not] prejudicial to amenity', even in areas with 'residential elements'. The AMC argued that gable-end advertising was 'one of the most obnoxious forms of advertising ... not consistent with good and orderly planning'. Echoing Manchester's remarks they added that it, 'inevitably accelerate[d] the deterioration' in districts that had either already 'begun to deteriorate' or did not 'possess high amenity value' in the first place.[74] The AMC's argument and Manchester Corporation's summation of the area in the Arthur Maiden judgement demonstrated the way authorities valued the control of the visual environment as a means of maintaining a certain degree of dignity and pride in an area, even where it was poor or scheduled for clearance. The Ministry saw things differently though, believing the burden of amenity still fell on showing some positive aspect of an environment, not preventing further disfigurement. Moreover, they insisted that 'advertising must be treated as an accepted feature of ordinary economic life, and there should be a good reason for refusing... applications to display advertisements'. Local corporations needed to concentrate on 'visual amenity' and not a much broader definition of 'psychological amenity', adding that they must consider the actual amenity of an area, rather than enforcing a blanket ban on gable-end advertising.[75]

The complexity of how the Ministry articulated their feelings about different types of amenity indicates just how malleable and unstable definitions associated with it were. Indeed, the instability of the new system had kicked a hornets' nest and local authorities who had often established settled, occasionally even cosy relationships with the dominant local advertising concerns found new problems emerging. In Suffolk, where a close and seemingly beneficial relationship with advertisers was detailed in an update on the first year of the new act, out of 76 applications, 49 were approved, 12 were approved with additional conditions and only 15 were refused.[76] Yet in Liverpool, since the 1947 Act had superseded their

[74] NA/HLG/71/1723, 'Meeting between AMC and Ministry', 4 May 1950.

[75] NA/HLG/71/1723, 'Memo from Mr Price-Jones to Mr Proper', 1 December 1949.

[76] NA/HLG/71/1723, 'Control of Advertisements', 2 September 1949, p. 1.

Table 5.1 Appeals by advertisers in Liverpool 1947–1949

Period	*Applications*	*Refused by corporation*	*Appeals made*	*Appeals allowed*
Year before 1 August 1948	194	103	13[a]	0
Year following 1 August 1948	258	136	129[b]	106

[a]Appeal made to Court of Summary Jurisdiction (usually the stipendiary Magistrate)
[b]Appeal made to the Minister of Town and Country Planning
Source NA/HLG/71/1723, 4 May 195

prized 1930 local corporation act in August 1948 the amount of applications to erect hoardings, the number of appeals and the number allowed had increased dramatically (Table 5.1).[77] In the summer of 1949, the Birmingham Town Clerk complained that the Minister's interpretation of appeals was undoing Birmingham's previously stringent control of advertisements, with seven out of ten appeals being allowed by the Minster.[78] A few months later Birmingham had approved 70% of the 215 applications they had received in the first year of operation, whilst only 21 reached the minister on appeal.

The heart of these disagreements did not stem from local authorities' misapprehension of economic reality—the figures, even in Liverpool, never show anything approaching repression of all advertisements—but from a differing perception of how the functioning of a city economy was enmeshed with ideas like residential amenity, civic pride or citizens' enjoyment of commercial spaces. As Ernest Baker has argued, outdoor advertising was abhorred by planners and civic boosters alike because it 'destabilised architectural and landscape design's power to properly form cities and citizens' but in post-war Britain, especially in the large industrial cities, there was often a certain sense of civic pride that went beyond architectural considerations of beauty.[79] In 1949 Birmingham Corporation recorded that they wished to preserve the appearance of their central throughfares, New Street and Corporation Street, and that they

[77] NA/HLG/71/1723, Notes on Meeting between Ministry and AMC', 4 May 1950.

[78] NA/HLG/71/1723, Notes on a conference with Birmingham, undated c. June 1949.

[79] Baker, 'Public Sites Versus Public Sights', p. 1197.

had always sought 'to keep the central shopping area of the city free from general commercial advertisements' even though 'there were no buildings of outstanding architectural merit and many had been war-damaged'. They were, however, rebuffed by Mr Price-Jones of the Ministry, who saw shopping streets as the most appropriate place for commercial advertising.[80] This sort of disagreement showed the Ministry misunderstanding the measurements of amenity which industrial cities like Birmingham perceived in their emblematic Victorian redevelopments as sites of civic display and municipal pride.[81] The Ministry's distinction between psychological and visual amenity, whilst vague, suggests that their notions of amenity were still firmly rooted in ideas of more discernible aesthetic value, but local authorities were plotting something that related more closely to maximising the order of public space and managing the quality of inhabitants' experience. Like Liverpool and Salford in the 1930s, the corporations of the post-war framed the commercialisation of lived space as an issue because it degraded the self-perception of their citizens through their everyday encounters with outdoor advertisements, not as an issue of subjective aesthetic quality.

The main areas where appeals were being sustained by the Ministry were typically working-class, often bomb-damaged residential areas. Katrina Navickas has shown that questions over the rights of working-class citizens to enjoy rural landscapes during the 1950s revolved around how sufficient levels of amenity value might be determined and how amenity might be defined, and here a similar process was at work.[82] In these teething troubles over the operation of the new act, it is tempting to frame the seeming insistence on the centrality of citizens' right to either civic areas or, particularly neighbourhoods free from commercial intrusion, as evidence of the spatial governance of post-war social-democratic state in operation. That, as Todd argues, no matter how flawed it might have been in delivery, in this period working-class citizens' 'interests were the state's primary priority' in urban development.[83] Indeed, a great

[80] NA/HLG/71/1723, Note on Meeting with Birmingham, 26 October 1949, p. 1.

[81] Andy Foster, *Birmingham: Pevsner Architectural Guides* (New Haven, 2002).

[82] Navickas, 'Conflicts of Power', p. 95.

[83] Selina Todd, 'Phoenix Rising: Working-Class Life and Urban Reconstruction, c. 1945–1967', *Journal of British Studies* 54:4 (2015), pp. 679–702 (p. 702).

deal of the records seem to show a concern for working-class experience and well-being. Sheffield's Cllr. Wood, for example, felt that the Ministry often thought that 'mixed areas [of industrial/commercial and residential use] so prevalent in northern towns' were suitable sites for advertisements.[84] This explanation has to, however, be tempered by the consideration of local authorities' longer-term activism against uncontrolled advertising, which also developed under both the leadership of Conservative and Liberal politicians. As Guy Ortolano has cautioned, the apparent markers of tendencies like market liberalism or social democracy might be better seen as constantly reshuffled elements of over time, rather than reading any particular creed as dominant or ascendant.[85] Indeed, one of the difficulties of understanding advertising control as a consistent tendency across two centuries is that it can at once stem from a deeply reactionary position on modernity that finds coincidental accommodation with aesthetic conservatism whilst also drawing support from liberal proponents of regulation and social democrats alike. Indeed, the further hardening of the stance of the Ministry against advertising under the incoming Conservative government of the 1950s cautions against seeing too much social-democratic fervour in advertising control.

Despite these reservations concerning the particular party-political flavour of the changes occurring, corporations' language of citizenship, amenity and public rights nevertheless illustrates a development in the rhetoric of spatial governance in the mid-century. In similar ways to how those who governed Victorian streets had seen the self-conscious freedom of the individual as part of the means to regulate their cities, here, local authorities imagined what I would cautiously term a 'social-democratic' subject. This citizen was conscious of both their own rights and the state's obligation to provide the greatest possible dignity and pleasantness in their everyday lives and environments. When, in late summer, the *Advertiser's Weekly* argued that changes in the pattern of decisions represented 'control becoming repression' and that local authorities were 'stretch[ing] beyond reason any interpretation of amenity' the Ministry clothed their response in the language of public consent.[86] They responded that they

[84] NA/HLG/71/1723, Notes on meeting between Ministry and AMC, 4 May 1950,.

[85] Ortolano, *Thatcher's Progress*. Thanks also to the author for discussions on this subject.

[86] 'Control Becoming Repression?', *Advertisers Weekly*, 24 August 1950, p. 1.

were subject to the censure of the people and there was, as yet, no 'indication whatever that public opinion sympathises with the advertisers'.[87] Advertising and billposting companies seem to have anticipated this turn, meeting with the Ministry on several occasions and stressing that there should be accommodation reached over areas of special control and the nature of amenity, but there was relatively little they could do and the direction of decisions was turning against them by 1950.[88]

Consideration of this imagined subject as the recipient of the benefits of the post-war state thus helps explain why changes in government seem to have had little impact on the trajectory of advertising controls. Lewis Silkin was replaced by Hugh Dalton in 1950, which signalled a distinct change in the character of appeals decisions. In 1949 60% of appeals to the Ministry were upheld, yet by the end of 1950 this fell to 23%.[89] In a directive to the civil service the new minister indicated that any decisions would lean more towards local authorities forthwith, suggesting an effort to show solidarity across the different levels of government rather than any specific dislike for outdoor advertising.[90] Dalton might have suggested that there would be no 'violent and sudden change in the trend of decisions', but civil servants calculated that under the new regime sustained appeals would fall to less than 8%. When they raised concerns over the administration of this, Dalton simply told them that they might be more successful if they tried harder.[91] In spring 1952 responding to billposting companies' insistence that 'amenity was never meant to cover some of the places' that local authorities, and now the new Ministry of Housing and Local Government, had decided it did, the transformation in opinion was made apparent. 'The Department', civil servant P.D. Coates wrote 'could in no circumstances accept that because people

[87] NA/HLG/71/1738, Untitled Note from T.H Sheepshanks, 31 October 1950.

[88] NA/AT/29/137, Meeting Between the Outdoor Advertising Industry Advisory Committee and the Ministry, 11 November 1949.

[89] NA/HLG/71/1723, Parliamentary question to Mr Dalton', 27 February 1951.

[90] NA/HLG/71/1738, 'Control of Outdoor Advertisements Directive on Future Administration' (from Dalton), 25 May 1950.

[91] NA/HLG/71/1738, 'Control of Advertisements – Principles Governing Appeal Decisions', 16 May 1950 and 'Control of Advertisements', 27 May 1950.

unfortunately enjoyed little amenity in their surroundings what amenity there was did not deserve protection'.[92]

The interpretation of how amenity related to individuals' experience of where they lived had become the primary consideration in advertising appeals. In contesting a denied appeal advertisers David Allen & Sons argued that given Crown St in Liverpool's 'industrial background...a poster panel of the type proposed could not but produce a pleasing relief to the existing drab and unsightly outlook'. In contrast the new Minister, Harold Macmillan, ruled that any advertising would be 'out of keeping with the residential character...and prejudicial to amenity' commenting particularly on the proximity of a group of 'pleasing' interwar flats.[93] Even the possibility of an advertising station being visible from a dwelling was enough to reject appeals too. In 1955 in Price Street, Birkenhead, despite there at the time being no residential properties, the Ministry rejected an appeal on the grounds that proposed future slum clearance might make any hoardings visible from local people's homes. Again, the advertiser's arguments that given the 'present drabness of this site...far from constituting any offense to amenity, the advertisement panels [would] relieve the existing harsh outlook' were out of step with the Ministry's opinion.[94] These cases represented several instances re-examined by the Ministry in 1956, who affirmed that though the cases were all in poorer areas, none of which had high amenity value 'in each case it was felt that large scale advertising was out of place and disfiguring, and likely to make the drab surroundings even worse for those who were living there'.[95] In 1936 in considering a case brought under the 1907 & 1925 ARAs the courts in Stoke-on-Trent had disagreed over how greatly nearby houses diminished the amenity of a rural landscape, yet twenty years later residential life was being depicted as the essence of amenity.[96]

[92] NA/HLG/71/1062, Correspondence: P.D. Coates to J.D. Jones, 28 May 1952.

[93] NA/HLG/71/1733, 'Site at Crown Street, Liverpool', Ref: 1324/40030/361, 6 June 1953.

[94] NA/HLG/71/1733, 'Site at Price Street Birkenhead', Ref: 954/40030/76, 27 June 1955.

[95] NA/HLG/71/1733, Note to the Minister, 20 April 1956.

[96] Scimgeour v. Stoke-on-Trent and North Staffordshire Billposting Co. Ltd. 22 April 1936, quoted in *The Solicitor's Journal*, 25 April 1936 unpaginated cutting in NA/HO/45/16607.

By the mid-1950s even when it was relatively obvious that local corporations were attempting to simply apply blanket restrictions on outdoor advertising, the Ministry lent their support. In Jarrow in 1955, in rejecting an application the local authority stated that the 'area, it is anticipated, will be re-developed at a very early date and that giving consent for even a short period would seriously impede the Council's programme...the time has arrived when a halt must be called to the display of advertisements in the Borough'.[97] Here the advertisers had proposed to somewhat beautify the spot, planning a paved forecourt with seating for the public, yet the Ministry simply pointed to the proximity of houses and rejected the appeal. The same year the Ministry discussed whether the powers of appeal might be dealt with locally and that the onus should shift so that the local decisions stood unless the Minister felt the 'circumstances were quite exceptional'. Furthermore, it was suggested that the designation of features worth protecting, on 'historical, architectural or cultural grounds' might also be stretched to include commercial and civic centres.[98] By 1956, of the 2029 appeals heard by the Ministry in the preceding year, only 32% were allowed, whilst the following year for posters alone the figure was 10%.[99] Victor Raikes, a quarter century after his appearance opposing the 1930 Liverpool Corporation Bill, wrote to the Minister on behalf of Arthur Maiden Ltd to complain that outdoor advertising permissions were being refused where a site was 'seen in conjunction with houses'. A situation Raikes described as unfair as it was nearly impossible to find sites that were not near houses, and that the 'economic interests of the country should ... be given just as much consideration in these matters as questions of amenity'. Enoch Powell, then the parliamentary secretary, responded that 'large advertisement displays are out of place in residential areas and even where the occasional house or group of houses survives among commercial development it seems to me generally right that advertising displays near the houses

[97] NA/HLG/71/1733, Site at 100/104 High Street Jarrow, Ref:1265/40030/12, 19 January 1955.

[98] NA/HLG/71/1738, Correspondence between Valentine and Downing c 20 January 1955.

[99] NA/HLG/71/1738, Note on response to question in Commons, 368/19955/6, 9 February 1956; Letter from H.H Mallatratt, 31 January 1957.

themselves should be at least restrained. There is nothing new in these views'.[100]

Advertisers contended that the Minister was 'falling over backwards' to support local authorities and instead of being umpire was part of the 'local authority machine' adding that 'local authorities and the Ministry where inventing amenity where none existed'.[101] Yet the Ministry was occasionally even going beyond the wishes of local government. In 1961 in Wells, despite an agreement being reached between Somerset CC, Wells CC and representatives of the trade and commercial interests concerning the coverage of an areas of special control made under the 1947 *T&CPA*, the Minister at the urging of his civil servants departed from the councils' wishes as 'illogical' and defined a larger area that included several sites regarded by all the local parties as commercial and the natural location for advertisements.[102] Advertisers, recognising that regulation now stood on a tipping point towards blanket licencing, did much to try and promote the civic values of their art and industry, even writing to ministers to show-off what they believed to be exemplary sites that improved the amenity of locations.[103] They continued to post before and after shots in their journal claiming that a coat of paint and a large sign could 'greatly enhance the amenities' of a formerly derelict wall. Public opinion did not smile on these attempts though: examining small gardens that advertisers had created to beautify billboard sites, architect Sir High Cason called them 'the ultimate hypocrisy', whilst artist and critic Stephen Bone likened the attempts to a 'gorilla with a lipstick'.[104] Demonstrating how great a change had occurred, the Ministry went as far as to criticise both the advertisers' best efforts and local authorities for not going far enough to protect amenity when rental incomes were of sufficient size.[105]

It is hard not to sympathise with the beleaguered advertising companies when reading the records of the Ministry. *Signs and Advertising*, a

[100] NA/HLG/71/1738, Correspondence between Raikes and Powell/Duncan Sandys, May 1956.

[101] 'NA/HLG/71/1738, Meeting with the Ministry of Housing and Local Government, 12 December 1956, pp. 1–2.

[102] NA/HLG/140/27, Various correspondence 1958–1961.

[103] NA/HLG/71/1738, Correspondence: G.R.Coles to Street, 2 August 1957.

[104] Turner, *The Shocking History of Advertising*, p. 250.

[105] NA/HLG/71/1738, Correspondence: G.R.Coles to Street, 2 August 1957.

billposters periodical, depicted the Wells judgement as one of the 'crazy, topsy-turvy difficulties' the outdoor advertisers now had to face. There was 'no justice or reason in the Minister's decision' this was 'a battle for advertising as a whole' against opponents who did not appreciate 'the important part advertising plays in our economic life'.[106] After years in which they had been able to count on negotiating with local authorities or appealing to central government as a final bulwark against local authorities' overreach, the reversal of fortune promised a difficult future. Responding to the Wells decision The Outdoor Advertising Council called it a 'travesty of administration', but an appeal to the Council on Tribunals was declined.[107] There is a palpable sense of panic in the repeated letters to the Minister throughout the 1950s from an industry that in 1937 had ebulliently claimed the industry was in such rude health that demand for space greatly outstripped that available, but was now faced with reduced space and, as advertising historian Terry Nevett concluded, was facing insurmountable challenges from press advertising and, from 1955, the television.[108]

Any attempt to recapture the former status quo proved futile. The way local and central government saw the functions of space and how the management of it facilitated their civic objectives had fundamentally changed. Indeed, though the changes of the early 1950s represented the point of greatest tension, the beginning of the 1960s represented the hardening of a system that was by now effectively licencing controlled by local authorities. In the late 1950s discussions concerning control of advertising turned gradually away from major breaches of amenity and moved towards the elimination of 'clutter'—essentially the uncontrolled nature of signage on shop fronts—which precipitated the *Town and Country Planning (Control of Advertisement) Regulations* 1960. These regulations clarified the conditions under which local authorities could limit the size and character of shop front advertisements and were

106 'Housing Minister Shocks the Outdoor Advertising Industry', *Signs and Outdoor Advertising* 15:12 (1961), p. 1. in NA/HLG/140/27.

107 NA/HLG/140/27, Letter from Outdoor Advertising Council, 28 April 1961; Letter from Council on Tribunals, 18 July 1961.

108 Nevett, *Advertising in Britain*, p. 191; Sheldon, *A History of Poster Advertising*, p. 99.

cemented by the restatement of the 1947 clauses in the 1962 *T&CPA*.[109] The advertising industry itself responded to the concerns over shop fronts in the same year, trying, as ever, to retain as much control as possible through self-governance—an approach favoured by the Ministry—with what became known as the 'Anti-clutter Code'. Indeed, despite reservations from parliament and an unsuccessful attempt to introduce further restrictive legislation in 1960, the code proved effective in removing c. 73,000 signs from shop fronts by 1962 and a further c.430,000 by 1970, almost certainly staving-off more stringent legislation.[110]

Conclusion

Attempts to further codify and expand advertising regulations did not end in 1960 or 1962 or, of course, in any other year. Yet around 1960 outdoor advertising legislation moved on to tackling either ever more detailed aspects of control or shifted to deal with the emergence of newer technologies of advertising. What the period that began in the interwar and culminated in what was effectively a system of licencing in the mid-1950s showed was the emergence and eventual dominance of a way of seeing, and thus governing, urban and suburban spaces, driven by ideas of planning, experience and framed by considerations of a social-democratic subject. By choosing this particular formulation of words I do not mean to imply that the sentiments of Salford or Liverpool or any of the other local authorities who sought dignity and amenity for their citizens were not genuine. Instead, my argument has suggested two conclusions. Firstly, that through the legislation and techniques of advertising control we can read the primacy of a way of looking at and governing urban space that was rooted in the languages of town planning and indicative of the patterns of urban modernism that emerged in the mid-twentieth century and shaped urban development and renewal until the 1970s. Second, that through the examination of the uses of

[109] *Town and Country Planning (Control of Advertisements) Regulations* (S.I. 1960 No. 695), s. 5, 8, 11 and 12 (1a) iv.

[110] Properly, the 'Code of Standards for Advertising on Business Premises' introduced by the Incorporated Society of British Advertisers. Hansard,, HC, 9 March 1962, vol. 655, cc. 767–843; History of Advertising Trust Chronology, online resource https://www.hatads.org.uk/documents/Chronology.pdf accessed 20 January 2021.

amenity we can see the centrality of a social-democratic subject—an individual possessed not only of self-conscious freedom, but of a knowledge of his or her rights to amenity, dignity and public space—to policies and approaches to governing space. The importance of this formulation is not that these invocations of amenity and the rights of citizens to residential or commercial areas free of outdoor advertisements are indictors of social democracy's triumph—although this book does not argue that they necessarily were not—but rather that the imagined social-democratic subject was a development in the toolbox of urban governance.

Urban modernism was characterised by a belief that the right sort of space was productive of order and functionality through the experience of it. It held that certain spaces not only contained the potential to create happier, healthier, more dignified citizens, but that these processes might be examined, become knowable and be spatialised in a distinct and profoundly functional way. The ultimate expressions of this lay, of course, in great projects of rebuilding. Urban modernism's logics were present in the glistening monuments to whichever architectural taste happened to capture the imagination of the planners at that time, but it represented much more than just style. It influenced calculations like the distance of homes from shops, the amount of green space, the colours of doors and garages and, indeed in permanent restrictions on advertisements and signs. Yet the often-unnoticed aspect of urban modernism was the way it seeped into systematic and holistic attempts to control and order extant spaces, even those that had no chance or need of actual rebuilding. The types of advertising control discussed here fall into this category. In unplanned, often run-down, working-class spaces, imagining the social-democratic subject involved contesting what amenity might mean, particularly in terms of the relative positive qualities of residential spaces. It meant imagining not how all subjects could become bourgeois or how architecture might civilise, but how all people might find and derive an experience of pleasantness in even the 'meanest' of streets.

Although in character this way of governing was the descendant of the liberal governmentality that had shaped public parks and houses in the late nineteenth century, it varied in seeking order and civility as a quality that nearly all places might have, and which should be preserved as a matter of governmental practicality. The social-democratic subject was not civilised and orderly because planners had produced a perfect world—although this was, of course, perhaps the pipedream endpoint of urban modernism—but because those who governed could be seen removing elements that degraded and disfigured, that assumed even the poorest environments had some amenity to someone. This is not to suggest that advertising control represented some nostalgic valorisation of the earthy simplicity of working-class life that needed to be protected; local authorities spent significant time defending areas they had already scheduled for slum clearance or places possessing a single house. They were not blind to the unpleasant nature of cramped terraced houses with damp walls, outdoor toilets and no heating, they would not have produced social housing in record numbers if they had been. Instead, the drive for advertising control was one of many small areas of control seized by local authorities in the period that demonstrates the quietly radical nature of their approaches to governing space. Approaches that stressed the potential for total control, were detailed, sought to manage all aspects of the environment and were local, mundane and deeply municipal in their outlook.

CHAPTER 6

Conclusion

Abstract The conclusions argues that the book has placed outdoor advertising control in Britain in its wider context, whilst providing a broad account of the passage of laws and attitudes that came to regulate, control and radically reduce the number of posters on the streets of Britain. The book speaks to the way that the interaction between commercialism and the purposes of lived spaces has been reframed. The conclusion contends that the most important contribution of the book is to show the ways that the twentieth-century state began to see all sorts of different spaces—from rural landscapes and ancient monuments to the streets in the industrial cities of the north—as having value to citizens. It concludes by arguing that more work needs to be done on the relationship between nuisance and amenity as concepts, suggesting that this may be a productive area for legal scholars to explore.

Keywords Posters · Billboards · Amenity · Governance · Legal

This book represents an attempt to put the history of outdoor advertising control in its wider context, whilst providing a broad—although

J. Greenhalgh, *Injurious Vistas: The Control of Outdoor Advertising, Governance and the Shaping of Urban Experience in Britain, 1817–1962*, Palgrave Studies in Economic History,
https://doi.org/10.1007/978-3-030-79018-9_6

I would allow, not exhaustive—account of the passage of laws and attitudes that came to regulate, control and radically reduce the number of posters, signs and billboards on the streets of Britain. That story alone has, I think, been worth telling because it speaks to the way that the interaction, sometimes antagonism, between commercialism and the purposes of lived spaces has been reframed over the last two hundred years. Nevertheless, the intellectual core of the book has tracked the emergence of an orthodoxy in the governance of space in Britain that lived environments could have a profound effect on the well-being and enjoyment of citizens and that they must be managed accordingly. The examination of these processes, particularly in Chapters 2 and 3, demonstrates the way that governments understood the important relationship between urban environments as sites for the functioning of capitalism, but also the way that the intrusions of the material manifestations of commercialism, like advertising vans or hoardings into lived environments had to be regulated. The book thus shows how outdoor advertising was civilised and ordered, paving the way in Chapters 4 and 5 for the discussion of how the state began to see the importance of controlling commercial elements from a much more intangible and experiential perspective, particularly in the places where people lived.

The most important conclusions of the book take place in these two chapters because they point to the ways that the twentieth-century state began to see all sorts of different spaces—from rural landscapes and ancient monuments to 'the meanest of streets' in the industrial cities of the north—as having value to citizens. Indeed, in the study of amenity the book suggests that there is still much that might be done to examine the corpus of legislation from the twentieth century that influenced how the state saw and governed space. This has interesting ramifications for everything from studies of town planning and housing provision to heritage legislation into the present that I hope this book might help other scholars examine. Over the period studied, outdoor advertising made contact with many different debates and approaches to governance, but the three central concepts that governed it were the elimination of nuisance and obstruction, the frameworks of liberal governmentality and finally the patterns of planning and urban modernism that characterised post-war urban development. Indeed, the examination of outdoor advertising control suggests that notions like nuisance and obstruction were constantly engaged with the processes of discipline and surveillance that defined what Patrick Joyce called liberal governmentality and expressed in the ways that advertisements had to be regulated to produce certain regimes of both physical and visual order. In notions like public nuisance and visual amenity—quasi-legal terms that leave space for imposition of order through interpretation—the study of outdoor advertising control illustrates the way that these regimes of control relied on public negotiations over meaning to function.

The interactions between nuisance and amenity which seem to me to be cousins of a sort are I hope, just one of many areas in which this book might stimulate further discussions. Reading the evidence of the judgements and the scoffing at SCAPA at the turn of the century can often give the impression that advertisers were merely voracious capitalists who wished to despoil every inch of the environment for commercial gain. Yet such a conclusion would be incorrect and have to ignore the great deal of productive, agreement-based civic politics that trade groups undoubtedly pursued in places like Suffolk and Birmingham, something that by their nature the files of central and local governments often only hint at. As I said in the introduction, this area of study would benefit from the examination of a really illuminating set of correspondence and minutes files from advertising companies or billposting associations. I have not been able to track anything like this down, despite some very helpful suggestions from people like the History of Advertising Trust, not least because many of the billposting firms have since been absorbed many times over into larger organisations. I have also deliberately only focused on SCAPA as the most effective of the organisations opposing advertising, though the CPRE holds files on this subject—particularly on their long and effective campaign to track and eliminate roadside advertisements—which did not find a home here. Omission here does not reflect a judgement about the importance of their work. The same might also be said of railway advertising, which occasioned great comment between the 1880s and 1910s, but gradually faded in importance over time, simply occasioning less comment. It appears that legislation governing rural advertising took care of a great deal of it, whilst advertising on railway premises continues to this day. It is possible that once hoardings on stations facing streets were curtailed under the mid-century acts they faded from attention, but I have yet to find compelling evidence to explain this change.

The final area that I have only really scratched the surface of is the notion of amenity. The importance of this concept to planning and management of extant spaces, whether in legal terms or in common discourse, cannot be underestimated. Legal scholars have made comment upon its qualities, but a forensic examination of it from the expert perspective of legal scholarship would be a tremendous boon to historians of urban experience, particularly this author.[1] I hope the book has conveyed how much weight seems to have become attached to the notion of amenity during the twentieth century and how fundamental it was to considerations of well-being and citizens' experience. Its appearance is essential to the formulation of what I have called the social-democratic subject. I do not mean this to be an entirely novel object of governmental practice; indeed, the social-democratic subject is really just the same individual that liberal governance sought to discipline through his or her own freedom. My formulation of the social-democratic subject read alongside amenity is an attempt to show how post-war urban modernism involved producing a specific variety of this figure. It involved imagining a citizen who was conscious of their rights to enjoy public space, who understood the role and perhaps duty of the state in encoding equality and dignity in the lived environment. Amenity was the jargon that meant the useful pleasantness of his or her environment and the right to experience it free of disfigurement, and outdoor advertising control was one of the tools that the state deployed to produce that.

[1] Philip Booth, *Planning by Consent: The Origins and Nature of British Development Control* (London, 2003), p. 61.

Bibliography

Primary Sources

Acts of Parliament

Act for the Good Government and Police Regulation of the Borough of Manchester, 1844 (7 and 8 Vict. c. 40)

Advertisements Regulation Act, 1907 (7 Edw. 7. c. 27)

Advertisements Regulation Act, 1925 (15 and 16 Geo. 5. c. 68)

Advertising Stations (Rating) Act, 1889 (52 and 53 Vict. c. 27)

An Act for vesting and securing the Lands of Muirhouse in the County of Lanark in General John Hamilton of Dalzell, 1833 (3 William 4, c. 6)

Ancient Monuments Act, 1931 (21 and 22 Geo. 5. c. 16)

Ancient Monuments Consolidation and Amendment Act, 1913 (3 and 4 Geo 5 c. 32)

Betting Act, 1853 (16 and 17 Vict. c. 119)

Betting Act, 1874 (37 and 38 Vict. c. 15)

Bill to facilitate Drainage of Lands in Scotland, 1847 (10 Vict. c. 11)

Burgh Police (Scotland) Act, 1903 (3 Edw. 7. c. 33)

Carlisle Corporation Act, 1887 (50 Vict. Sess. 2. c. 19)

Central London Railways Act, 1891 (54 and 54 Vict. c. 196)

Chester Improvement Act, 1884 (47 and 48 Vict. c. 239)

Corrupt and Illegal Practices Prevention Act, 1883 (46 and 47 Vict. c. 212)

Housing Act, 1923 (13 and 14. Geo. 5, c. 24)

Housing, Town Planning etc. Act, 1909 (9 Edw. 7. c. 44)

J. Greenhalgh, *Injurious Vistas: The Control of Outdoor Advertising, Governance and the Shaping of Urban Experience in Britain, 1817–1962*, Palgrave Studies in Economic History,
https://doi.org/10.1007/978-3-030-79018-9

Huddersfield Improvement Act, 1871 (34 and 35 Vict. c. 151)
Local Government Act, 1948 (11 and 12 Geo. 6 c. 26)
London Hackney Carriage Act, 1853 (16 and 17 Vict. ch. 33)
London Streets Act, 1762 (2 Geo. 3. c. 21)
London Streets Act, 1763 (3 Geo. 3. c. 23)
London Streets Act, 1764 (4 Geo. 3. c. 39)
London Streets Act, 1765 (6 Geo. 3. c. 54)
London Streets Act, 1765 (5 Geo. 3. c. 50)
Metropolis Local Management Act, 1855 (18 and 19 Vict. c. 120)
Metropolis Management Amendment Act, 1862 (25 and 26 Vict. c. 102)
Metropolitan Paving Act, 1817 (57 Geo. 3. c. 29)
Metropolitan Police Act, 1839 (2 and 3 Vict. c. 47)
Municipal Election (Corrupt and Illegal Practices) Act, 1884 (47 and 48 Vict. c. 70)
Railway Fires Act, 1905 (5 Edw 7. c. 11)
Rating and Valuation Act, 1925 (15 and 16 Geo. 5. c. 90)
The London Building Act, 1894 (57 and 58 Vict. c. 213)
The London County Council (General Powers) Act, 1893 (56 and 57 Vict. c. 221)
The London Sky Signs Act, 1891 (54 and 55 Vict. c. 78)
The Metropolitan Board of Works Act, 1877 (40 and 41 Vict. c. 8)
The Towns Improvement Clauses Act, 1847 (10 and 11 Vict. c. 34)
Town and Country Planning (Control of Advertisements) Regulations (S.I. 1960 No. 695)
Town and Country Planning (Control of Advertising) Regulations (S.I. 1948 No. 1613)
Town and Country Planning Act, 1932 (22 and 23 Geo. 5. c. 48)
Town and Country Planning Act, 1947 (10 and 11 Geo. 6, c. 51)
Town Planning Act, 1925 (15 and 16 Geo. 5, c. 16)

Archives

British Library
BL/PP1092baa, SCAPA Quarterly Papers: New Series
BL/PP1092bac, SCAPA Pamphlet Collection
Hansard
House of Commons
HC, 16 June 1851, vol. 117
HC, 1 August 1859, vol. 155
HC, 12 June 1851, vol. 117
HC, 14 February 1934, vol. 285
HC, 14 June 1907, vol. 176
HC, 20 April 1874, vol. 218

HC, 27 July 1933, vol. 280
HC, 7 August 1862, vol. 168
HC, 9 March 1962, vol. 655
House of Lords
HL, 19 May 1922, vol. 50
HL, 4 March 1924, vol. 56
HL, 8 April 1889, vol. 334
HL, 9 June 1853, vol. 127
House of Commons Papers
Twenty-sixth report of the Commissioners for Making and Maintaining the Caledonian Canal, 13 July 1830, 668, vol. 15 VX.111
Select Committee on Police and Sanitary Regulations Bills: Special Report, Proceedings, 5 July 1895, vol. 12, XII.113
Journals of the House of Commons (1688–1834), 21 May 1827, 8 Geo IV, vol. 82
Special report from the Select Committee on Local Legislation, 1929–30, No. 163, vol. 6
London Metropolitan Archives
LMAA/SCA Society for Checking Abuses of Public Advertising, 1892–1952 archive
LMA/A/SCA/01/001, Minute Book 1911–1922
LMA/A/SCA/01/003, Minute Book 1910
LMA/A/SCA/01/004, Minute Book 1935–1953
LMA/A/SCA/03/002/001, 'America' file
LMA/A/SCA/03/002/005, 'Correspondence with Local Authorities B'
LMA/A/SCA/03/002/010, 'Europe' file
LMA/A/SCA/03/002/017, Correspondence with Local Authorities 'L'
LMA/A/SCA/03/009/009, 'Automobile' file
LMA/A/SCA/03/009/014, 1913 Advertisements Regulation Bill
LMA/A/SCA/04/003, 'Membership'
LMA/A/SCA/05/004/020, 'Hereford Byelaws 1927'
LMA/A/SCA/06/002/005, 'Roadside Advertisements (Northern Area)'
Mass Observation Archive
MOA, 'Reactions to Advertising', December 1938
MOA, 'Public Attitudes to Advertisements', February 1944
National Archives (Kew)
NA/AT/29/137, '1968 Advertising Appeals Abolition'
NA/HLG/140/27, 'Somerset CC Control of Advertisements 1958'
NA/HLG/54/264, 'Liverpool Corporation Bill 1930'
NA/HLG/56/1116, 'Rating and Valuation – ADVERTISING STATIONS (1932 to 1968)'

NA/HLG/71/1045, 'Advertisement Regulations under Town and Country Planning Bill 1947: Consultations with Trade Interests'
NA/HLG/71/1062, 'Meetings and Discussions on Advertisement Control Generally'
NA/HLG/71/1723, 'Advertising Control, 1948 Onwards'
NA/HLG/71/1733, 'Display of Advertisements within Buildings, 1948–1968'
NA/HLG/71/1738, 'Appeals Policy'
NA/HLG/79/421, 'Advertisements: Moss Lane West: Appeal by Arthur Maiden Limited'
NA/HO/45/16607, 'BYELAWS: Advertisement Regulation Byelaws: General Papers'
NA/HO/45/17318, 'BYELAWS: London County Council: Advertisements'

Online Sources

Historic England, *The Setting of Heritage Assets* (2nd edition) https://historicengland.org.uk/images-books/publications/gpa3-setting-of-heritage-assets/heag180-gpa3-setting-heritage-assets/ accessed 20 February 2021.
History of Advertising Trust Chronology https://www.hatads.org.uk/documents/Chronology.pdf accessed 20 February 2021.

Newspapers and Periodicals

A Beautiful World: The Journal of the Society for Checking the Abuses of Public Advertising
Aberdeen Evening Express
Aberdeen Free Press and Journal
Aberdeen Herald and General Advertiser
Advertisers Weekly
Alloa Advertiser
The Auckland Star
The Billposter
Birmingham Daily Post
Bradford Daily Telegraph
Brighouse News
Brighton Gazette
Bristol Times and Mirror
The British Architect and Northern Engineer
The British Architect
The Builder
Canadian Law Journal
Chatham News and North Kent Spectator

Clerkenwell News
Daily Telegraph and Courier
Devizes and Wiltshire Gazette
Dover Express
Edinburgh Evening News,
Elgin Courant, and Morayshire Advertiser
The Era
The Field
Folkestone Express, Sandgate, Shorncliffe & Hythe Advertiser
The Globe
The Graphic
Hastings and St Leonards Observer
Hertford Mercury and Reformer
Holborn Journal
Household Worlds
Huddersfield Daily Examiner
Illustrated London News
The Ipswich Journal
Islington Gazette
Lambeth and Southwark Advertiser
Lancaster Guardian
Leamington Spa Courier
Leeds Mercury
Leicester Chronicle
Lincolnshire Chronicle
Liverpool Echo
Liverpool Mail
Liverpool Mercury
Lloyds Weekly Newspaper
London City Mission Magazine
London Evening Standard
Loughborough Monitor
Manchester Evening News
Marylebone Mercury
The Morning Advertiser
Morning Chronicle
Morning Post
National Review
Newtonards Chronicle & Co. Down Observer
The Northern Star
Oxfordshire Weekly News
Punch or the London Charivari

Railway News and Joint Stock Journal
Saint James's Chronicle
The Saturday Review of Politics, Literature, Science, and Art
The Scotsman
Sheffield Daily Telegraph
Sheffield Telegraph
Shoreditch Observer
Signs and Outdoor Advertising
Solicitor's Journal
The Sporting Gazette
St James's Gazette
Suffolk and Essex Free Press
Teesdale Mercury
The Times
Waterford Mirror and Tramore Visitor
Weekly Freeman's Journal
West London Observer
West Middlesex Advertiser and Family Journal
West Middlesex Gazette
Western Mail
Whitstable Times and Herne Bay Herald,
Wigan Observer and District Advertiser
Wolverhampton Chronicle and Staffordshire Advertiser
World's Press News and Advertisers' Review
Wrexham Advertiser
Yorkshire and Leeds Intelligencer
Yorkshire Post and Leeds Intelligencer

Published Primary Works

Abercrombie, Patrick and Johnson, T.H. *Sheffield and District Regional Planning Scheme* (Liverpool, 1931).

Balfour of Burleigh, Lord. *Report of the Royal Commission on Local Taxation*, 1901, C.D. 638.

Bullock, Edward. *The Law Journal Reports*, 1877 (London,1877).

Burn, James Dawson. *The Language of the Walls: And a Voice from the Shop Windows, or, the Mirror of Commercial Roguery* (London, 1855).

Carlyle, Thomas. *Past and Present* (London, 1843).

Davidge, William. *The Rotherham Regional Planning Scheme* (Rotherham, 1925), p. 102.

Dickens, Charles. *The Complete Works of Charles Dickens: Reprinted Pieces, Vol. III* (New York, 2009).

Evans, Richardson. *The Age of Disfigurement* (London, 1893).
Evans, Richardson. 'Advertising as a Trespass on the Public', *The Nineteenth Century* 37:220 (1895), pp. 968–980.
Evans, Richardson. *An Account of the SCAPA Society* (London, 1927).
Gray, W. Forbes. 'Letters of Some Old Scots Jurists', *Juridical Review* 36:4 (1924).
Larwood, Jacob and Hotten, John Camden. *The History of Signboards, from the Earliest Times to the Present Day* (London, 1908 [1866]).
Moran, Clarence. *The Business of Advertising* (Abingdon, 1905).
Schlesinger, Max. *Saunterings in and about London* (London, 1853).
Sheffield Town Planning Committee. *Sheffield Replanned* (Sheffield, 1945).
Sheldon, Cyril. *A History of Poster Advertising* (London, 1937).
Simmel, Georg. *The Metropolis and Mental Life* (1903).
Smith, William. *Advertise, How? When? Where?* (London, 1863).
Stead, William T. *The Art of Advertising. Its Theory and Practice Fully Described* (London, 1899).
Unknown Author. *Tommy Toddless Comic Almenac* (sic) (Leeds, 1865).
Vale, Edmund. *Ancient England: A Review of Monuments and Remains in Public Care and Ownership* (Malvern Wells, 1941).

Published Secondary Material

Altick. Richard D. *Punch: The Lively Youth of a British Institution, 1841–1851* (Columbus, 1997).
Applegate, Celia. *A Nation of Provincials: The German Idea of Heimat* (Berkeley, 1990).
Assael, Brenda. 'Art or Indecency? Tableaux Vivants on the London Stage and the Failure of Late Victorian Moral Reform', *Journal of British Studies* 45:4 (2006), pp. 744–758.
Baigent, Elizabeth. '"God's Earth Will Be Sacred": Religion, Theology, and the Open Space Movement in Victorian England', *Rural History* 22:1 (2011), pp. 31–58.
Baker, Laura. 'Public Sites Versus Public Sights: The Progressive Response to Outdoor Advertising and the Commercialization of Public Space', *American Quarterly* 59:4 (2007), pp. 1187–1213.
Baker, Richard Anthony. *British Music Hall: An Illustrated History* (Barnsley, 2014).
Bernstein, David. *Advertising Outdoors: Watch This Space!* (London, 1997).
Booth, Philip. *Planning by Consent: The Origins and Nature of British Development Control* (London, 2003).
Booth, Philip. 'The Control of Discretion: Planning and the Common-Law Tradition', *Planning Theory* 6:2 (2007), pp. 127–145.

Booth, Philip. 'Planning and the Rule of Law', *Planning Theory and Practice* 17:3 (2016), pp. 344–360.

Bowler, Catherine and Brimblecombe, Peter. 'Control of Air Pollution in Manchester Prior to the Public Health Act, 1875', *Environment and History* 6:1 (2000), pp. 71–98.

Boyes, Georgina. *The Imagined Village: Culture, Ideology and the English Folk Revival* (Manchester, 1993).

Briggs, Asa. *The Age of Improvement, 1783–1867* (London, 2014).

Brimblecombe, Peter. *The Big Smoke: A History of Air Pollution in London Since Medieval Times* (London, 1988).

Bullock, Nicholas. *Building the Post-war World: Modern Architecture and Reconstruction in Britain* (London, 2002).

Chandler, James. *Explaining Local Government: Local Government in Britain Since 1800* (Manchester, 2007).

Cherry, Gordon. *Cities and Plans: The Shaping of Urban Britain in the Nineteenth and Twentieth Centuries* (London, 1988).

Churchill, David. *Crime Control and Everyday Life in the Victorian City: The Police and the Public* (Oxford, 2017).

Colls, Robert and Dodd, Philip (eds). *Englishness: Politics and Culture 1880–1920* (London, 1986), pp. 160–202.

Conekin, Becky, Mort, Frank and Waters, Chris (eds). *Moments of Modernity: Reconstructing Britain, 1945–1964* (London, 1999).

Confino, Alon. *The Nation as a Local Metaphor: Württemberg, Imperial Germany and National Memory 1871–1918* (London, 1997).

Conway, Hazel. *People's Parks: The Design and Development of Victorian Parks in Britain* (Cambridge, 1991).

Corbett, David, Holt, Ysanne and Russell, Fiona (eds). *The Geographies of Englishness: Landscape and the National Past 1880–1940* (New Haven, 2002).

Cregoe, Mathew and Readman, Paul (eds). *The Land Question in Britain, 1750–1950* (Basingstoke, 2010).

Cronin, Anne M. *Advertising Myths: The Strange Half-Lives and Images of Commodities* (London, 2004).

Crook, Tom. 'Sanitary Inspection and the Public Sphere in Late Victorian and Edwardian Britain: A Case Study in Liberal Governance', *Social History* 32:4 (2007), pp. 369–393.

Cullingworth, Barry and Nadin, Vincent (eds). *Town and Country Planning in the UK* (London, 2002).

Daunton, Martin (ed). *The Cambridge Urban History of Britain, Vol. 3 1840–1950* (Cambridge, 2000).

Daunton, Martin. *Just Taxes: The Politics of Taxation in Britain, 1914–1979* (Cambridge, 2002).

Davis, Tracy C. 'Sex in Public Places: The Zaeo Aquarium Scandal and the Victorian Moral Majority', *Theatre History Studies* 10 (1990), pp. 1–13.

Elliott, Blanche B. *The History of English Advertising* (London, 1962).

Ewen, Stuart. *Captains of Consciousness: Advertising and the Social Roots of Consumer Culture* (New York, 1976).

Foley, Donald L. 'British Town Planning: One Ideology or Three?', *The British Journal of Sociology* 11:3 (1960), pp. 211–231.

Foster, Andy. *Birmingham: Pevsner Architectural Guides* (New Haven, 2002).

Fraser, W. Hamish. *The Coming of the Mass Market, 1850–1914* (London, 1981).

Gold, John. *The Practice of Modernism: Modern Architects and Urban Transformation, 1954–1972* (London, 2007).

Greenhalgh, James. *Reconstructing Modernity: Space, Power and Governance in Mid-Twentieth Century British Cities* (Manchester, 2018).

Gunn, Simon. 'The Rise and Fall of British Urban Modernism: Planning Bradford, Circa 1945–1970', *Journal of British Studies* 49:4 (2010), pp. 849–869.

Hamlin, Christopher. 'Nuisances and Community in Mid-Victorian England: The Attractions of Inspection', *Social History* 38:3 (2013), pp. 346–379.

Harrison, Bryan (ed). *The History of the University of Oxford. Volume VIII: The Twentieth Century* (Oxford, 2004).

Hasegawa, Junuchi. *Replanning the Blitzed City Centre: A Comparative Study of Bristol, Coventry and Southampton* (Buckingham, 1992).

Hewitt, John. 'The "Nature" and "Art" of Shell Advertising in the Early 1930s', *Journal of Design History* 5:2 (1992), pp. 121–139.

Hewitt, John. '"The Poster" and the Poster in England in the 1890s', *Victorian Periodicals Review* 35:1 (2002), pp. 37–62.

Hewitt, John. 'Designing the Poster in England, 1890–1914', *Early Popular Visual Culture* 5:1 (2007), pp. 57–70.

Hilton, Matthew. *Consumerism in Twentieth Century Britain* (Cambridge, 2003).

Houck John W. (ed). *Outdoor Advertising: History and Regulation* (London, 1969).

Howkins, Alun. *The Death or Rural England: A Social History of the Countryside Since 1900* (London, 2003).

Iveson, Kurt 'Branded Cities: Outdoor Advertising, Urban Governance, and the Outdoor Media Landscape', *Antipode* 44:1 (2012), pp. 151–174.

Jackson, Mark. *The Age of Stress: Science and the Search for Stability* (Oxford, 2013).

James, Michael F. *Construction Law* (London, 1994).

Jerram, Leif. *Streetlife: The Untold History of Europe's Twentieth Century* (Oxford, 2011).

Joyce, Patrick. *The Rule of Freedom: Liberalism and the Modern City* (London, 2003).

Keller, Lisa. *Triumph of Order: Democracy and Public Space in New York and London* (Chichester, 2009).

Kent, Christopher A. 'Review: Thomas Richards, The Commodity Culture of Victorian England', *Victorian Periodicals Review* 25:3 (1992), pp. 145–147.

Larkham, Peter J. 'Thomas Sharp and the Post-war Replanning of Chichester: Conflict, Confusion and Delay', *Planning Perspectives* 24:1 (2009), pp. 51–75.

Loxham, Angela. 'The Uses and Abuses of Public Space: Urban Governance, Social Order and Resistance, Avenham Park, Preston c.1850–1901', *Journal of Historical Sociology* 26:4 (2013), pp. 552–575.

Madgin, Rebecca and Rodger, Richard. 'Inspiring Capital? Deconstructing Myths and Reconstructing Urban Environments, Edinburgh, 1860–2010', *Urban History* 40:2 (2013), pp. 507–529.

Mandler, Peter. 'Against "Englishness": English Culture and the Limits of Rural Nostalgia, 1850–1940', *Transactions of the Royal Historical Society* 7 (1997), pp. 155–175.

Matless, David. *Landscape and Englishness* (London, 1998).

McKendrick, Neil, Brewer, John and Plumb, J.H. *The Birth of the Consumer Society: The Commercialization of Eighteenth-Century England* (Bloomington, 1982).

Meller, Helen. 'Urban Renewal and Citizenship: The Quality of Life in British Cities, 1890–1990'. *Urban History* 22:1 (1995), pp. 63–84.

Mosley, Stephen. *The Chimney of the World: A History of Smoke Pollution in Victorian and Edwardian Manchester* (London, 2009).

Navickas, Katrina. 'Conflicts of Power, Landscape and Amenity in Debates over the British Super Grid in the 1950s', *Rural History* 30:1 (2019), pp. 87–103.

Navickas, Katrina. 'Keep Britain Tidy: From Public Health to Patriotism in the Twentieth-Century Campaign Against Litter', *Unpublished Paper*, 2021.

Nead, Lynda. *Victorian Babylon* (London, 2000).

Nelson, Richard and Sykes, Anthony Edward. *Outdoor Advertising: Its Function in Modern Advertising and Marketing* (London, 1953).

Nevett, Terry. *Advertising in Britain: A History* (London, 1982).

Nixon, Sean. *Hard Sell: Advertising, Affluence and Transatlantic Relations, c.1951–69* (Manchester, 2013).

Offer, Avner *Property and Politics, 1870–1914: Landownership, Law, Ideology and Urban Development in England* (Cambridge, 1981).

Ortolano, Guy. Thatcher's *Progress: From Social Democracy to Market Liberalism Through an English New Town* (Cambridge, 2019).

Otter, Chris. 'Making Liberalism Durable: Vision and Civility in the Late Victorian City', *Social History* 27:1 (2002), pp. 1–15.

Popple, Simon and Toulmin, Vanessa (eds). *Visual Delight: Essays on the Popular and Projected Image in the Nineteenth Century* (London, 2000).

Readman, Paul. 'Landscape Preservation, "Advertising Disfigurement", and English National Identity c.1890–1914', *Rural History* 12:1 (2001), pp. 61–83.

Readman, Paul. 'Preserving the English Landscape, c.1870–1914', *Cultural and Social History* 5:2 (2008), pp. 197–218.

Richards, Thomas. *The Commodity Culture of Victorian England: Advertising and Spectacle, 1851–1914* (Stanford, 1990).

Rose, Nikolas. *Powers of Freedom: Reframing Political Thought* (Cambridge, 1999).

Saumarez Smith, Otto *Boom Cities: Architect Planners and the Politics of Radical Urban Renewal in 1960s Britain* (Oxford, 2019).

Schutt, Stefan, Roberts, Sam and White, Leanne (eds). *Advertising and Public Memory: Social, Cultural and Historical Perspectives and Ghost Signs* (Abingdon, 2017).

Scott, Geoffrey R. 'The Cultural Property Laws of Japan: Social, Political, and Legal Influences', *Washington Law Journal* 12:2 (2003), pp. 314–401.

Sheldon, Cyril. *A History of Poster Advertising* (London, 1937).

Slack, Paul. *The Invention of Improvement: Information and Material Progress in Seventeenth-Century England* (Oxford, 2015).

Smith, H.L. (ed). *War and Social Change: British Society in the Second World* (Manchester, 1986), pp. 58–77.

Speakman, Malcolm V. *Shell's England: Corporate Patronage and English Art in Shell Posters of the 1930*s (PhD Thesis, University of Manchester 2014).

Spencer, David. 'Pulling Out of Colleges and Landed Property: The Oxford Colleges and the Church Commissioners', *Area* 32:3 (2000), pp. 297–306.

Spencer, J.R. 'Public Nuisance—A Critical Examination', *Cambridge Law Journal* 48:1 (1989), pp. 55–84.

Stein, Richard. *In Victoria's Year: English Literature and Culture, 1837* (Oxford, 1996).

Sullivan, Alvin. *British Literary Magazines: The Victorian and Edwardian Age, 1837–1913* (London, 1984).

Szczepanowska, Hannah M. *Conservation of Cultural Heritage: Key Principles and Approaches* (London, 2013).

Taylor, Charles R. and Chang, Weih. 'The History of Outdoor Advertising Regulation in the United States', *Journal of Macromarketing* 15:1 (1995), pp. 47–59.

Taylor, James 'Written in the Skies: Advertising, Technology and Modernity in Britain Since 1885', *Journal of British Studies* 55:4 (2016), pp. 750–780.

Thornton, Sara. *Advertising, Subjectivity and the Nineteenth-Century Novel Dickens, Balzac and the Language of the Walls* (London, 2009).

Tiratsoo, Nick. 'The Reconstruction of Blitzed British Cities, 1945–55: Myths and Reality', *Contemporary British History* 14:1 (2000), pp. 27–44.

Todd, Selina. 'Phoenix Rising: Working-Class Life and Urban Reconstruction, c.1945–1967', *Journal of British Studies* 54:4 (2015), pp. 679–702.

Turner, Ernest *The Shocking History of Advertising* (London, 1965).

Vorspan, Rachel. 'Freedom of Assembly and the Right to Passage in Modern English Legal History', *San Diego Law Review* 921 (1997), pp. 927–1042.

Waine, Peter and Hilliam, Oliver (eds). *22 Ideas That Saved the English Countryside: The Campaign to Protect Rural England* (London, 2016), pp. 186–197.

Walkowitz, Judith. *City of Dreadful Delight: Narratives of Sexual Danger in Late-Victorian London* (Chicago, 1992).

Walton, John K. 'Towns and Consumerism', in Martin Daunton (ed), *The Cambridge Urban History of Britain, Vol. 3 1840–1950* (Cambridge, 2000), pp. 715–744.

Weeks, Jeffrey. *Sex, Politics, and Society: The Regulation of Sexuality Since* 1800 (London, 1989).

Weinstein, Ben. 'Questioning a Late Victorian "Dyad": Preservationism, Demolitionism and the City of London Churches, 1860–1904', *Journal of British Studies* 53:2 (2014), pp. 400–425.

Wickham, Chris. *The Inheritance of Rome: A History of Europe from 400 to 1000* (London, 2010).

Wiener's, Martin. *English Culture and the Decline of the Industrial Spirit* (Cambridge, 1981).

Wildman, Charlotte. *Urban Redevelopment and Modernity in Liverpool and Manchester, 1918–39* (London, 2016).

Wischermann, Clemens and Shore, Elliott (eds). *Advertising and the European City: Historical Perspectives* (Aldershot, 2000).

Index

J. Greenhalgh, *Injurious Vistas: The Control of Outdoor Advertising, Governance and the Shaping of Urban Experience in Britain, 1817–1962*, Palgrave Studies in Economic History,
https://doi.org/10.1007/978-3-030-79018-9

The manufacturer's authorised representative in the EU is Springer Nature Customer Service Centre GmbH, Europaplatz 3, 69115 Heidelberg, Germany. If you have any concerns regarding our products, please contact ProductSafety@springernature.com

Printed and bound by CPI Group (UK) Ltd, Croydon, CR0 4YY

30/09/2026

02225466-0016